I hope that everyone who reads this book will find a new challenge and a happy life.

Steve Kim

Winning 60 out of 60 battles

AMERICAN DREAM

AMERICAN DREAM

STEVE Y. KIM FOUNDATION
3530 Wilshire Blvd #380
Los Angeles, CA 90010

Published by the STEVE Y. KIM FOUNDATION
First Edition, Oct 1, 2019

ISBN 979-11-5776-779-3 (03800)

A CIP catalogue record of the National Library of Korea for this book is available at the hompage of CIP(http://seoji.nl.go.kr/) and Korean Library Information System Network(https://kolis-net.nl.go.kr/) (CIP2019037804)

The proceeds from selling this book are used for the nonprofit organizations.

Winning 60 out of 60 battles

AMERICAN DREAM

Written by Steve Kim

Where happiness comes from?

Prologue

When I returned to Korea in 2007, I wrote a book titled, *Steve Kim's Dream, Hope, Future Story*. With this opportunity, my life and experiences were known to many people and I was very busy lecturing in many places. During that time, I learned the sad reality of the youth and I set up 'Dream Hope Future Leadership Center' to help save them.

I recently acquired a golf course in Santa Clarita and crossed back over to the United States. Upon my return, I met with many locals and most of them wondered who I was and why I took over a failing golf course. As they learned about my plans to develop the resort, their curiosity about me grew even bigger.

In order to share my vision with them and help them understand where I came from, I decided to publish a book.

Dream, Hope, Future Stories, which was first published in Korea, was revised to include why I came back to the United States and what I want to accomplish in the future.

I hope my *American Dream* will bring new challenges and inspiration to my readers, and I hope that I can devote my passion to find meaningful work.

September 2019

Steve Kim

Contents

CHAPTER 3

How Could Success Be Possible?

CHAPTER 4

Where Happiness Comes From

CHAPTER 5

Meaningful Life in Korea

CHAPTER 6

Noblesse Oblige

CHAPTER 7

Return to the Land of Opportunity

CHAPTER 8

Last Wishful Venture

CHAPTER 1

Seeking Hope

A humble beginning

I was born in 1949 in Seoul, Korea. At that time, Korea was very poor because it had just liberated after 35 years of Japanese colonial rule. The country had never been industrialized and cultivation of rice fields was the main source of income.

Due to the conflict between ideologies that occurred during the process of establishing an independent government, the

The view of Seoul right after the Korean War

Korean War broke out in June 1950. The whole nation fell back into chaos and the people lost everything. Thanks to the active participation of U.S. and UN forces, the war ended in 1953, and the country was divided into South and North Korea.

Like many others, my father lost everything during the war. When the war ended, he tried with all his effort to recover financially but he was unable to bring himself out of poverty. When I was 10 years old, my parents, three older sisters, and my younger brother rented a small room in a house on an orchard located just outside of Seoul. There was no electricity and my seven family members couldn't eat properly. After school, my friends and I used to satisfy our hunger by picking fruits on an open orchard.

I attended an elementary school in a small town with only 120 students. After graduating, I passed the entrance exam and entered the prestigious 'Kyungbok Middle School'. This created a lot of buzz because no one from our town had ever achieved this before.

One day, while I excitedly waited for the entrance ceremony, my mother gave me my sister's old school uniform that she herself mended to fit me. Although I didn't say anything about it to my mother, I felt ashamed and resentful that we couldn't even afford a new school uniform.

A desperate goal planted by my mother

My mother was a graduate of the prestigious Kyeonggi Girls' High School, even though it was very rare for a woman to receive a modern education at that time. Unfortunately, she suffered from epidemic meningitis during the Korean War and continued to suffer aftereffects. Despite her pain and discomfort, she was so diligent that she swept and wiped the house all day long.

Since my father failed in business and had no income, she had a hard time raising my five young siblings. Whenever I saw my mother struggling, I wanted to do something to help but there was nothing I could do. I thought to myself, 'The only thing I can do is study. I should study harder and make my mother proud!' From that moment on, I poured all my efforts into studying thinking that nothing could be more difficult than my mother's hardship.

As a result of my efforts, I scored the highest grades and ranked first at my school. As soon as I got my report card, I ran home and shouted, "Mother, I won first place!" My mother saw my report card and said, "My son is amazing, I am so proud of you!" I felt rewarded and was determined to succeed and give my mother a life of comfort.

After middle school, I was accepted into the prestigious 'Kyungbok High School,' which everyone envied. However, as the time for college approached, I began worrying about expensive tuition fees. Even my older sisters had to give up their college studies due to our family's financial hardship. I thought, 'As the oldest son, I'm the only one who will be able to financially support my struggling poor family, so wouldn't I have to go to college? But how am I going to pay for my tuition when I go to college?'

One day, while spending a few days with resentful feelings towards my parents, cadets of the Korea Military Academy came to our school in nice uniforms to promote their admission. The moment I saw their bright and energetic appearance, I thought 'This is it! When I enter the academy, I don't have to worry about my tuition!' It seemed as if my worries and concerns would be solved in a flash.

I applied to the Korea Military Academy and passed the written exams without any difficulty. However, I failed the physical examination because my lower jaw was protruding. With disappointment and frustration, I studied for another year and entered the Department of Electronic Engineering at Sogang University in 1969. At the time, Sogang University was a small university with about 1,000 students and an electronic engineering department was established for the first time that year.

The late 1960s was the early days of the electronics industry when digital watches and black-and-white TVs were just beginning to emerge. There was no specific information on my major, but I thought if it was a new and promising field, I could easily get a job after graduation.

When the semester began, however, the list of subjects to be taken included subjects such as Korean, Social studies, Biology, and Chemistry, which I did not take well to even in middle school and high school. While other friends were immersed in their major studies in the laboratory, I enjoyed my free and liberal college life doing things I wanted to do, such as tennis and volume dance. In the blink of an eye, four years passed and I graduated from college and joined the army.

Entrepreneurship discovered in the army

After a set period of time at the military training camp, I was assigned to the Airborne Unit. I applied for the brigade's tennis coaching position, but since the commander didn't have much time to play tennis, I was given the responsibility to run a small surplus store in the unit.

The store provided services such as putting soldiers' gear on uniforms, repairing uniforms, and selling things that weren't handled by the Post Exchange Store such as sportswear and souvenirs. I had never been in business before but I always wondered, 'What do soldiers need? How can I increase sales?'

After some thought, I began stitching 'Airborne Special Forces' labels on taekwondo robes and sold them. I also made an album with pictures of Airborne jumping off the plane and playing taekwondo. This album became a big hit so whenever soldiers went on vacation, they took the album with them. I also brought red bean steamed buns and milk into the store, which were not handled before.

Every day, the store was very crowded with soldiers who became hungry for snacks after hard training. When I ran out of supplies, I would take a handcart and go out of the unit to buy from the civilian stores to resell. This unexpected experience of running a military surplus store became a valuable lesson, which helped me a great deal with my startups in the U.S. later on.

Bound for the United States

When I finished military service, there weren't many jobs I could apply for because Korea was still not industrialized. My friends went to research institutes or went through masters and doctorate courses to become university professors, but that didn't suit me.

At that time, my oldest sister Ockhee was living in the U.S. after she married an American who worked in Korea. A few years later she invited my parents to the U.S., so they moved to Los Angeles. When my sister heard that I had trouble finding a job in Seoul, she called and said, "You should come over to the U.S. and you can become an engineer after you earn a master's degree." It seemed there would be a lot more employment opportunities in U.S. than in Korea, so I made up my mind to go. To learn English before my move, I studied hard by repeatedly listening to American radio.

While I was waiting for my immigration VISA to the U.S., one of my friends introduced me to a girl who was a college senior. At first glance she looked attractive and I thought it could be easier to settle in America together. So, we got engaged in Korea just before I left for the U.S.

In 1976, when I was 27 years old, I finally got on airplane to America. When I arrived at Los Angeles airport, my sister was there to meet me. Leaving the airport, I saw countless cars driving on the highway and realized that I was in a country completely different from Korea. 'What can I do here? How can I survive?' Contrary to expectations I had before leaving Korea, fear flooded in.

While staying at my parents' house, I started looking for places to work and eventually got a job at an autopart warehouse in Carson. I was so happy to find a place to work even though I was only making $2.50 an hour. The job was to stock various auto parts on the shelves all day. It was a very tough and laborious job but I put in all my effort and worked very hard. Whenever there were opportunities to work longer hours or to work on weekends, I didn't mind taking on the work for additional income.

My fiancé arrived in LA about six months later and we rented a small apartment for $150 a month near California State University in Los Angeles, where I started my graduate program majoring in Electronics. It was very difficult to work during the day and attend school at night. To catch up in school and get accustomed to a new life wasn't easy. I wished I could only concentrate on studying to quickly become an engineer but I was unable to quit working because I didn't qualify for a student loan.

My brother-in-law who married my second oldest sister was running a ceramic pottery factory in Paramount. On weekends, I sold defective flowerpots from the factory at the flea market to make additional money and eventually worked as a supervisor at the factory.

Then, to gain some experience in a field related to my studies, I joined Kratos in Pasadena as an electronic technician and earned $6 an hour. Sometime later, I worked as a test engineer for Burroughs, a company that made large computers, and earned $8 an hour. Finally, in 1979, after three long years of hard work and study, I earned a master's degree in electronics engineering. During that period of my life, I felt like time had stopped and I was stuck in a long tunnel!

American Dream became reality

When I left for the U.S. in 1976, my goal was to become a design engineer and live comfortably with my family. After graduation in 1980, I joined Litton Data System in Van Nuys as a design engineer making $12 an hour. My American Dream became a reality!

By taking out a bank loan, my wife and I bought a small house in east LA for $30,000. It had two small bedrooms and a small garden. I was so happy to own a house to take care of and groom with my own hands.

My parents were also very happy seeing what their son had accomplished despite growing up in poverty and struggling to settle in the United States. My father was so proud that he wrote letters to his many friends in Korea, but unfortunately passed away soon after due to arteriosclerosis. I was sad and regretful that he couldn't live long enough to see my bigger successes down the road.

Litton Data System specialized in designing Command Control Systems, which could command warfare. There were more than 500 engineers with many years of experience. Although I studied in graduate school, I had to learn from scratch. I didn't expect to be assigned important tasks, but I was eager to learn and work harder than others to handle bigger tasks as soon as possible.

Nevertheless, the project itself was so large and fragmented that it would take years to complete, and I couldn't move ahead alone. I had to do what was assigned to me, without knowing the whole process or seeing the big picture. I started to feel that I was a small part of a big engine and began to lose the motivation to learn and work hard.

I dreamed of becoming an engineer in America because I wanted to have a stable and comfortable living. However, once I became an engineer, I wanted to learn faster to get ahead of others and live better. After the disappointment, I was unhappy and started to worry about what I would do next.

I wondered to myself, 'if I moved to a small company, would I be able to learn more things at a faster pace?' At the same time, I worried about the possibility of being given a job that I haven't done before and being unable to manage it. But wasn't this the kind of burden and responsibility I've been longing for?

CHAPTER 2

Endless Challenge for a Better Life

Turning point of my life

In the summer of 1981, I made up my mind to move to a small company and began searching for a job in the Los Angeles Times. I found a company, Phalo Optical Systems in Chatsworth, who was looking for a project engineer to be in charge of product development. After a lengthy interview, I was hired for the position. They had only 30 employees with a small factory next to the office.

Back then, copper wire was used to transmit data between buildings but the distance and the bandwidth was limited. In early 1980, there was a paradigm shift from copper wire to fiber optic cable in data communication. I happened to join the company that was dealing with this new technology.

I was given the responsibility of designing a small fiber optic data communication system. I had to learn the entire product development process from the beginning. It was totally new to me but luckily there was another engineer who I could learn from.

After the product was released to the market, I had to wear the System Engineer's hat and traveled with sales people for site visits because I had more knowledge on the product than anyone else in the company. Because our products need to interface with a variety of computers, I used to go to the field and fix them if there was a compatibility problem. This gave me an opportunity to broaden my scope of responsibilities beyond just a project engineer.

When I was moving from a large company to a small company, my goal was to learn more and learn faster but here, I was given a chance to learn manufacturing, application engineering, sales support and after-service. When I finished my first project I was assigned to another project which allowed me to learn even more. I was so excited to learn something new every day.

Originally, my role was to be in charge of developing the product, but I flew all over the country, engaged in technical support, and assisted in sales. In small companies, one person often has to do many things, making it easy to get involved with other departments and understand how they work.

Since the company was small, everything I did was exposed naturally and the president always kept an eye on me. He always praised me and it made me feel good to be recognized. As a result, he gave me a big raise and my salary doubled in three years since becoming an engineer at Litton Data Systems.

A reckless challenge

I always had a curiosity of how the products were utilized in the field and I wanted to learn about a few other competing products in the market. I took a close look at the competing product specifications and tried to find out how our products differed from those of other companies.

Naturally, I began to speculate what products our customers would need in the future. Companies must plan new product developments ahead of time and make timely preparations, but I was never given an opportunity to present new product ideas to the company.

As time went on, I came up with a brilliant idea of how customers could save money. I immediately began to explore the idea at my spare time. It took me a while to convince myself that my product concepts offered significant competitive product advantage over existing products in the market at that time.

During the two and a half years that I worked at Phalo, I gained experience in product development, manufacturing, and learned how the products were sold and serviced. This was only possible because all those activities happened under one small roof and I was engaged in each of those different functions. In addition, I had a chance to directly interface with key customers such as Sandia National Lab, Grumman Data Systems, Lockheed and NASA.

At that time, startups were uncommon. I was very scared of starting my own, but I couldn't control my strong impulses. I asked myself, 'If I give up now and do nothing, wouldn't I regret it for the rest of my life?' I shared my thoughts with three other friends who were working as engineers at other companies.

"The product I'm envisioning can send a lot more data at once, which can save customers a lot of money. I've done all the analysis of other competitors."

"Really? Are you sure you can do it? How can I help you?"

"Can you each invest $30,000 on my new venture? I think I could build the prototype with the money and if I show it to venture capitalists, I could convince them to make investments for launching the products."

"I know there are a lot of challenges ahead but I think it's worth the risk. If it succeeds we all could make a lot of money"

They invested $30,000 each and I added $10,000 to make up the startup capital. In a garage attached to one of their houses, the office was set up with two assembly tables, lights, and telephones. At that time, $100,000 was about a one-year salary for a corporate executive. It wasn't a small amount of money, but when I bought some equipment that I needed, I didn't have much left.

My colleagues who invested helped me after work, but I had to do most of the work on my own. I had to do everything from designing, ordering parts, building prototypes, testing and etc. I worked almost 24 hours a day in the garage. It was too much work, but I couldn't afford to hire help. At that time, I felt like I was trapped in a long tunnel. Almost one year went by when I finally finished the working prototype to demonstrate in front of investors.

An unexpected crisis

I realized that I didn't know where to find investors or how to make contact with them. When I entered the garage I thought it would be easy to find investors once I had a prototype to show them. Eventually, all initial capital for the startup was exhausted. If I couldn't attract more money quickly, all my efforts would go to waste.

In the mid-1980s, the IT industry was not active yet. There wasn't much concept of entrepreneurship, and there were not many venture capital companies that would provide working capital. I realized that I needed a business plan to get their attention but I hadn't seen one nor did I know how to write one. I needed someone who had done this before but I didn't know how to find one.

In order to start a business, I realized that I had to rehearse myself not only with the product ideas but also with various other factors including the plan for raising the working capital.

Later, I asked myself 'If I had known that there were this many variables to form a successful startup beforehand, would I dare to really start a new venture?' There is a proverb that 'even though the sky collapses there is a way to escape'.

In my desperation, I thought of Dick Bass who was the president at Phalo. I gave him a call and invited him to the garage. He was very surprised to find what I had done after I left the company.

"Dick, why don't you join me as a vice president of sales and marketing? I will share 10% of the company with you, which could become a lot of money if we pull it off together." After long consideration, Dick said, "Okay, Steve, let's do it. I think we'll have a good chance of making it happen." We shook hands and from that moment I had an American partner to work with.

Soon after, Dick introduced me to Paul Hope, a retired CFO who worked at GTE. He had a lot of experience in business operations and wrote the new business plan. When I first met him, I felt as if he was looking down on me, thinking 'how would a young Asian with no business experience succeed in venture?' Regardless, I passionately explained to him about the market opportunities, competition, advantages and differentiation from other competitive products. After much persuasion, Paul finally decided to make an investment into my venture with the condition of him being one of the board members.

Later, he told me that he was very impressed with me because he had never seen any startups put together a prototype before looking for investors. Paul would have never imagined that his decision at the time would make him 2,500 times a return through two of my ventures.

Paul introduced me to many angel investors in Southern California. Angel investors were those whose net worth were over $1 million and could take a risk investing in high risk startups. Whenever I met new prospects, I passionately persuaded them to draw investment decisions and through them I was introduced to one after another. At last, in over two and a half months, I raised $300,000 from 30 angel investors. I was exhausted and learned a very valuable lesson of how difficult it was to raise money from investors. I decided that I would no longer reach out for more money and I would definitely succeed with $300,000.

Dick Troop, a lawyer, Trude Taylor, a former CEO, and Paul Hope became directors of the board when they made investments in the company. I didn't know the role of board members at that time, but later I learned that I would need to get their approval for all important decisions and they could fire me if I didn't perform. So actually, they became my bosses

First at bat – home run

When I started Fibermux, the goal was to grow the company and make it profitable. I moved my office to a 1,500 square foot warehouse-style building and hired seven employees for product development, production, A/S and accounting. I had to step in for sales because we couldn't wait until we found someone for the position.

First, I visited NASA in Huntsville, Alabama and met Frank, the purchasing manager who I met while working at Phalo.

"Frank, I can show you a new product that can save you a lot of money because you can simultaneously send more data using a pair of fiber."

"How is that possible? If you leave your equipment here, I will check it out and see if what you are saying is really true."

In about two weeks we received an order for 10 units from NASA. The first order was worth $100,000. 'Wow, NASA really placed an order? I can't believe it! It's incredible that my vague ideas have actually become a reality.' It was a moment that I put together with a little money in a small garage and proved it could really happen! The time of blood, sweat, and tears passed by just like a movie and I was thrilled!

Our products had very high added value, resulting in 80% operating margins and we could make $80,000 operating profit from NASA's first order. While it could take a few years for the newly established company to break even, we could be profitable from the start. I still believe this is unprecedented in the history of any ventures. It was a miracle!

I called Frank at NASA and said, "Thank you so much for believing in us. Would you mind if I used you as a reference?" With a strong reference on hand, I was searching for the next possible prospects.

Soon after, I visited Larry, the purchasing manager of Grumman Data System in New York. I tried to convince him of the competitive advantage over the product he was using, but he said that even though my product looked superior, it would be difficult to change to another vendor. Weeks later, I received an unexpected call from him.

"Steve, the product we just bought from one of your competitors doesn't work. A field engineer from the manufacturer came out to fix it but he couldn't figure out what was wrong. Can you help me out?" He sounded desperate over the phone.

"Larry, I will fly out tonight and visit tomorrow morning."

"Steve, you're coming in person?"

"Don't worry about it. I have no one else to send right at this moment."

I hung up the phone and flew to New York that evening. Whenever I went out to troubleshoot the problems in the field, I had to carry a heavy Oscilloscope with me. After a couple of hours troubleshooting, I found the problem was that the switch setup was done incorrectly because it was mislabeled. After this, Grumman data system became a loyal customer.

Once they became our clients, I called or visited in person to make sure that they were happy with our products and services. At the same time, I wanted to find out their future needs.

One of our clients, Sandia National Lab in New Mexico, was a giant company developing nuclear bombs. Peter, a senior engineer responsible for IT services, had always been friendly and kind to me. Whenever I would visit him, I asked what kind of product functions and features he would want in the future. The conversations I had with Peter, who was a brilliant visionary, helped me come up with new product ideas.

As a result, I launched a new product called '**Magnum**,' which could tie up to 8 buildings with one pair of fiber and could mix and match with many interfaces. It was versatile and became a breakthrough in fiber optic data communication. It allowed

Celebrating the release of Magnum at an IT show

Fibermux to become number one in the market just three years after its founding.

In 1990, Fibermux posted $50 million in annual sales and net profit of $10 million. This took only six years since its inception. To achieve that, we had to overcome numerous obstacles beyond description.

I never studied management and I had no experience in managing a startup. My experience was only in product design and manufacturing. I had to learn hiring, putting together an organization, setting up business objectives and budget and many more things from scratch. I was not afraid to ask and consult with anyone and relied on my common sense. I tried to motivate employees with good pay and stock options.

The fiber optic data communications market was a niche market and growth was limited. Nevertheless, I had to set aggressive goals every quarter and somehow achieved them without exception. The board members were very pleased with my performance.

Fortune favors the prepared mind

Once the company became profitable for many quarters, investors expected to get their investment back. This could be done by either selling the company or by listing it on NASDAQ. The board had to make a decision.

To sell the company, we would have to put it on the market but the customers would find out and future sales could be adversely affected. To be listed on the NASDAQ, we had to convince ourselves that we could show growth for the foreseeable future. The stock would plunge if it failed to meet the growth expectation after going to NASDAQ. In the end, we decided to list it on NASDAQ. Amidst our preparations, the war in the Middle East broke out in 1990 and we had to withdraw the plan because the stock market plunged.

One day, the president of ADC Telecommunication who manufactures fiber optic cables, made an unexpected visit to meet me.

"As you know, we're trying to expand our business into data communications but we don't want to start fresh. I'm here to find out if you are willing sell the company. We looked around and I was convinced that your company could be the best fit for us."

"Are you telling me that I should sell Fibermux to you? As you have probably heard, we're preparing to list on NASDAQ."

"I know, but wouldn't we be able to grow bigger and faster through our sales network after the merger?"

Since I had constant pressure of growth and returning profit to original investors, I entertained his idea of a merger. After a month of push-and-pull negotiations, the company eventually sold for $54 million.

In six years from its humble start in 1984, investors made 25 times return on their investment. They were very happy and I became a hero! This was the result of the pure pressure and struggles of meeting quarterly goals and everyone's dedication and commitment to making it happen.

I was asked to stay and work as CEO for two more years after the sale. I made $10 million and it was a lot more money than I ever imagined, but all that excitement didn't last very long. I began to think about what I was going to do in two years after leaving the company. 'Isn't it too early for me to retire at the age of 45? Should I find a job as a CEO at another IT company?'

In hind sight, I had a lot of regrets of the past six years. I could have reduced a lot of trial and error if I had some experience running a company. Many people told me that what I had achieved was amazing, but to me it was only half a success.

One day, Yuri Pikover, who worked for me as a Western regional sales manager at Fibermux came to see me. Whenever he had problems that he couldn't solve on his own, he always came to ask for help. I liked him a lot because he was smart, aggressive, and always exceeded my expectations. He bluntly asked,

"Steve, what are you going to do when you leave the company?"

"Well, I've been thinking about that a lot lately."

"Wouldn't you want to try another startup?"

"Another one? You know how difficult it was, yet you want me to do it again?"

"At that time, it was hard to raise the capital, but if you do it again, investors will line up for you. You have a proven record and they want you to do it again".

"Doing it the first time is always a challenge but second time will be much easier."

"Do you really believe that?"

"Absolutely! Please don't waste the hard earned experience you gained from Fibermux."

That incident triggered my heart and I started to dream of a new challenge.

A distinctly different start

In the late 1980's, there was a huge paradigm shift in the IT industry. Personal Computers(PC) were introduced by Apple & IBM and they began to replace many computing tasks performed by Mainframes and Mini-Computers. As a result, there were new needs for PCs to be interconnected. Then, the personal computers could be connected and create Local Area Network(LAN).

LAN HUB was introduced to connect various PCs in one location and it required many HUBs to be connected in order to create a larger HUB. Every agency, bank, school, and so on, needed these HUBs and it created a fairly large market. The problem was that the network slowed down when too many computers were sharing a 10 Megabyte(MB) Ethernet HUB, and it caused 'bottleneck'.

Switching-LAN, which provided 10 MB Ethernet connection to every PC, could alleviate the bottleneck of the LAN HUB regardless of how many computers were connected. I predicted that the Switching-LAN market could be huge.

Xylan, my second startup venture. was born in July 1993. The business goal was to become a leader in the Switching-LAN market. The beginning of Xylan was totally different from the humble beginning of Fibermux.

When investors heard that I started a new venture, venture capitalists and former investors flocked in to make an investment. I only took $5 million for initial working capital. I set a very ambitious goal and wanted to not only be a market leader but also wanted to quickly grow the business and list on NASDAQ within three years.

I put most my emphasis on hiring talented engineers. From my experience with Fibermux, I learned that the success or failure of business depends on recruiting good people and utilizing them properly. Recruiting talented engineers was critical in order to develop sophisticated products faster than others and to gain a first-mover advantage in the Switching-LAN market. However, it wasn't easy finding competent engineers because they were working elsewhere with stable jobs. I diligently searched around through people I knew.

Whenever I found a good candidate, I had to convince them by passionately portraying my vision. I spared no money in recruiting excellent talents by offering them a much higher salary and stock options for all employees. Later, those engineers who joined me early on became millionaires.

John Bailey, who became vice president of engineering, was a key hire. I asked around to all engineers I had known in the past,

"Who do you think is the most qualified person to lead Research and Development (R&D) of Xylan?" I eventually learned that John Bailey, who was the head of R&D at Timeplex, a phone switch manufacturer, could be the best candidate for the job. When I met him, he looked like a very sincere, trustworthy and capable young man. But most importantly he was very technical even though he didn't graduate college.

"John, I desperately need someone like you. Together, we could build a very exciting company which could lead us to huge success."

"Well, I have a lot of responsibilities with my current job but I might be able to help you whenever you need my advice."

I couldn't give him up easily, so I met him a few more times and repeatedly persuaded him. Six months later, he finally joined me as the vice president of engineering.

When John decided to join our company, ten more engineers who worked for him also followed. He not only led the engineering team but he became my right hand man. We strategized together regarding any important business matters and whenever I ran into business issues he was the first one I consulted with. I could hardly imagine the success of Xylan without John Bailey.

Every time I interviewed someone for a new hire, I told them "We have too much work to do but we can't hire good people fast enough. Sometimes you might have to work a lot more than

40 hours a week. If you join us and work hard, we can become successful and you could make a lot of money from the stock option."

In less than six months, we hired over 30 talented engineers and used up most of the $5 million I initially raised. I raised another $10 million to build a structure to support the growth of the company.

I was so surprised to find that I became a bold and aggressive businessman. This might be because I was too confident about the future business outlook and was able to visualize that early on. It was a big contrast to the Fibermux days when I was conservative in spending due to fear that business could slow down and we would need money to endure the hard times.

After a year and a half of product development, Xylan introduced a new product called **OMNI SWITCH**. Xylan's initial product offering garnered huge attention in the LAN industry. The products had capability and versatility that no other competition could offer. Since the products had so many

Signing ceremony for OEM agreement with IBM executive

sophisticated functions and features, the barrier to entry was extremely high.

As soon as the product came out, global companies such as IBM, Alcatel, Fujitsu and Hitachi lined up to sell our products using their brands. The demand for the product was so high that it was difficult to keep up with supply. However, we could not solely rely on them to get our products to the market. We had to expand our own sales network in a hurry.

I learned that branding and first mover advantage was very critical in the high tech industry. Yuri was traveling around the world to major cities, including London and Paris, and tried to recruit sales people and local distributors. I helped him out by traveling to Seoul and Tokyo and other major cities in Asia.

Just two years since Xylan was founded, the revenue exceeded $30 million in the fourth quarter of 1995. I could easily predict that sales in 1996 could exceed over $120 million. I called a board meeting and told them,

"I think now is the best time to go to NASDAQ. I am confident we can grow over 300% next year and double the growth in the following year. As you know, we are recognized as the number one LAN Switching company and the market for it will be further explored by the industry. The valuation of the company is measured by the growth rate not by the current revenue."

"Steve, are you really confident?"

"Have I ever not delivered what I promised you in the past? You're well aware I never missed my quarterly objective since I founded Fibermux."

To go to NASDAQ, the company must first select an investment bank(IB). Then, the IB performs due-diligence to make sure all the materials presented by the company are correct. They hire experts in various fields and check out the market, competition, legal & accounting records, customer references who are using the products and etc.

We hired Morgan Stanley as our prime investment banker. They put together a detailed plan for the road show. Then, I toured New York, San Francisco, Dallas, London, Paris and a few more major cities with the CFO to hold company briefings to institutional investors.

During the road show, we had to move on a very tight schedule because we had many meetings lined up in each city we visited. Sometimes we had to fly via private jets to meet the schedule. It was quite a tense, nerve wracking, and exciting experience.

I could never forget the presentation I made at the historic Astoria Hotel in Manhattan, New York. When I arrived there, over 100 people were waiting for me. I tried to get my message across by pointing out a few important messages:

- How I accomplished unprecedented success at Fibermux after a humble start out of a garage.
- How I became a savvy businessman and established Xylan as a market leader in such a short time.
- Xylan's product, OMNISWITCH's very high barrier to entry.
- Our dominant position in exploring the market.
- How we are aggressively setting up our own sales channel.
- How Xylan's revenue will grow exponentially.

At that time, I didn't look sophisticated and I couldn't speak well in front of the audience. All I had was passion and conviction!

On March 12, 1996, Xylan was listed on NASDAQ. That morning, everyone involved gathered at Morgan Stanley's office in San Francisco and watched how the stock market would react after the road show.

At the opening, the stock price started much higher than expected and it ended at $54 per share, which was 100% higher than the initial offering price. It was the 3rd biggest debut in NASDAQ history at that time and it made a huge splash in the stock market. It had been less than three years since I founded the company, and its value had reached as much as $3 billion. I couldn't believe what was happening in front of my eyes.

20 years ago, I came to the U.S. and my humble dream was to become an engineer. It wasn't easy achieving that dream. After becoming an engineer, I realized that I had a passion for pursuing a better life and not just having a stable job. That led me to the reckless startup, Fibermux, and after that I put in every effort you could imagine due to my fear of becoming a failure.

After Xylan's phenomenal debut on NASDAQ, investors' expectations grew very high and my responsibility for exceeding their expectations also doubled.

Listed companies are required to announce expected annual sales and profits in advance. All of the company's strategies are exposed as if they are in a crystal bowl and the CEO's ability is also evaluated by stock price. Most importantly, the performance of the company is measured by quarterly results of revenue and profitability, which is linked to share prices. For example, if the market predicts a net profit of one dollar per share but it is short a penny, the share price could fall by 10-20%.

I could hardly imagine how all the shareholders and employees, who were also the shareholders of the company, would react if their assets reduced significantly because I couldn't meet quarterly goals. I was never at ease because another quarter was always waiting at the end of every quarter.

When the company grew bigger in size it was much more difficult to increase revenue by over 10% each quarter. When the new quarter began we might have only 50-60% of orders on hand and we had to book the remaining orders and deliver them before the quarter was over.

We had over 400 sales people spread in 25 offices around the world. They all promised they could generate a certain amount of orders before the quarter ended but I couldn't sit still and wait for it to happen. So, I personally visited many sales offices to assist in closing the deals. In order to save time, I often flew at night or over the weekends. Sometimes I visited five countries in a week.

Our products were very complex and had many options to choose from. Many of them went into production after the order was received and we also had to arrange all necessary parts to be able to build them in time to meet quarterly numbers. In addition, many things could go wrong, so I couldn't stop thinking about it until the end of the quarter.

The company grew steadily as it continued to struggle every quarter. It required hiring more people to support the growth. A number of new products had to be developed to meet the market demands. In 1999, the total number of employees grew to over 1,000 people and they were spread over many locations.

As the organization became increasingly fragmented, it was difficult to communicate efficiently. I felt as though control and efficiency deteriorated over time. In addition, I noticed that product developments were missing the schedule, which could be detrimental to the future growth of the company. I was tired and frustrated!

Although I had 12 vice presidents working for me I felt like I was alone. Regardless, I had to meet the revenue goals quarter after quarter. I should have never set such high expectations in front of investors at the road show. I learned later that setting low expectations and exceeding them little by little could have been much easier for managing the growth of the company. I wished someone had taught me this lesson before the company went public.

Bill Gates of Asia

One day in early 1999, the President of communications division at French conglomerate Alcatel and the Chief strategy officer visited.

"What's the purpose of the visit?"

"I'd like to discuss the merger of Alcatel and Xylan. I think the synergy between the two companies will be big in many ways..."

Alcatel was Europe's largest telecommunications company for many years and it entered into the data communication market for a few years before Xylan. When Xylan came out with new products, Alcatel branded our products with their name and successfully marketed them in Europe. The merger was proposed as a strategy to become a world leader by combining Alcatel's voice technology and Xylan's data communication technologies. On the surface, I pretended to be calm, but I was happy to think that I could release my huge burden if the merger was successful.

After more than a month of negotiations, we agreed to the deal at $2 billion.

The media was in an uproar after the signing of a merger deal between Xylan and Alcatel as it was rare for such a huge transaction at that time. Prestigious dailies and magazines, such as The Wall Street Journal, Time Magazine, and Business Week covered "The Story of Xylan achieved by Steve Kim", as their main stories. One of the media quoted me as the 'Bill Gates of Asia'.

Winning 60 out of 60 battles

As a result of the sale of Xylan, original investors made 100 times return on their investments and many Xylan employees became millionaires. For those who believed in me from the start and invested in both start-ups, they earned about 2,500 times return. I, the major shareholder, also made big money and everyone around me became rich.

1999, Celebrating the sale of Xylan with Alcatel's President

Managing a high-tech company is no different than a war without guns. We have to fight every quarter and meet the goals for shareholders. Technology is changing so fast and new startups will surprise you with new guns much more powerful. We had to predict the market change and be prepared for it. If not, you could be outpaced overnight.

There lived a Korean admiral, Sunshin Lee, who fought the war against the Japanese invasion in the 15th century. He fought against them 23 times in six years but he won every single battle and saved the country from a very inferior condition.

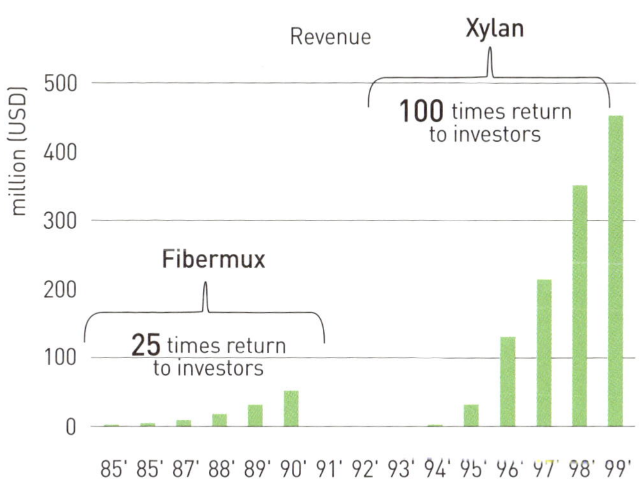

I fought 60 quarters during the 15 years of running two companies and never lost a battle. 'How important is the wisdom of knowing when to descend? How important is it to realize where you are?'

After the sale of Xylan, the IT bubble began exploding in early 2001 and many high-tech enterprises suffered. If I had not been able to make a decisive decision at that time, would I have possibly made it through the crisis?

CHAPTER 3

How Could Success Be Possible?

Trusted CEO

Appeared in Arirang TV (YouTube, Heart to Heart EP2654)

After completing both startups successfully, the major media in Korea portrayed me as the main character of a new myth in the IT industry, and many people came to me and asked,

"How is it possible that you succeeded in the U.S. when it's even difficult to do so in Korea?"

"Well, I'm not sure! I didn't learn business in school nor did I have experience in business. But whenever I ran into something

I didn't know, I wasn't afraid to ask around to find the solution. To me, business is common sense."

"But you must have something very unique from others behind your tremendous success. Can you tell me what it is?"

"When you are running a business, you cannot do it alone. It is very important to work together with employees in unison.

Upon arriving in the U.S., I worked at a few different places before I joined a small company. I looked back at my time working as an employee with those companies and tried to find what made me happy and what made me dissatisfied. I learned that to be productive, self-motivation was more important than money. So I tried to find what would motivate my employees."

Mentoring class for entrepreneurs

Management to maximize efficiency

In order for a company to maintain high growth, it must have a solid organization. It is important that each employee is placed in the right place so that he/she can generate the best results without wasting time. An employee who is reluctant to do things only produces 50% of their capacity, while an employee who is motivated could produce 200% of his potential. When I worked in a large company, I was very unhappy because there was no sense of belonging or presence in the company.

When Xylan reached its maximum size, there were over 1,000 employees in 25 offices around the world. With so many employees spread in different areas, we needed a system to efficiently communicate with each other no matter where they were.

Therefore, I implemented a system that allowed me to find out what was going on no matter where I was. All the employees had to write their weekly status reports to their manager, then share the reports with their team members. All the team leaders then wrote me weekly reports and shared them with other team leaders. The weekly report explained what they did that week and what they had to do the following week. If there were any issues or problems, they should explain why.

Instead of having regular staff-meetings, I held many meetings while I was in the office to strategize on certain plans or to find solutions for issues that were unresolved. I called only those people who were necessary for the meeting and held meetings in my office with short notice (ad-hoc meeting). Often times, we had heated discussions, but I tried to end with amicable results. In the process of bringing each other's thoughts together, we were able to maintain the team spirit in the company.

In addition, whenever I found time in the office, I walked around areas and approached individuals on the floors. "Hello, Mark. How are you? How is the project you're working on? Are they coming along well? Do you see any problems with the meeting schedules? Is there anything I can help you with? Are you happy with the job?"

Rather than placing an emphasis on reporting formats and procedures, I tried to have casual conversations to create more intimacy. I tried to create a culture of enhancing employees' sense of belonging and creativity, which in turn resulted in efficiency throughout the corporation.

Recognition and reward

Before I became a CEO and worked as an employee, I wanted to work harder and earn more money than others. At the same time, I wanted to get attention and recognition from others. With that in mind, I tried hard to motivate all of my employees to work for themselves. I tried to remind them how important their work was and how it could affect the whole business.

I had all-hands meetings with all the employees once a quarter and shared what was going on with the company. I shared the results of past quarters and goals for upcoming quarters. I told them what our challenges were for meeting those goals.

I kept my door open (open-door policy) for all employees, which allowed them to approach me easily with any suggestions for the improvement of the company. As a result, I was able to hear their concerns or the problems I would otherwise have been unaware of. Just by listening to them, we were able to increase their presence and pride in the company.

I introduced the MBO(Management by Objectives) method. Before the end of each quarter, 40 different team leaders presented their next quarter goals, which had to be weighed by the objective and had to be measurable. At the end of the quarter, each team leader turned in MBO results and were paid bonuses based on their own performance evaluation. This assured me that they were focused on goals in line with the company's objective.

At that time, I paid a higher salary than other companies to attract talent and gave stock options to all employees. I hoped that the stock options made them feel like they were working for their own business. Many of them became millionaires when we listed on NASDAQ.

Recently, I met a former employee of Xylan at the Country Club. We chatted about the days we used to work together and I asked about his two daughters and his current affairs. He told me,

“I benefited so much not only for me, but for my family as well.”

“It’s been a long time since then. Anyway, I’m happy to see you healthy and doing well.”

“It’s true. Thanks to you, I was able to send my two daughters to good colleges and was able to help them buy new homes. They are now married and have children so my wife and I are happy without any worries. Many other employees who worked for you are thankful for what you have done for them.”

“I’m happy to hear that. At that time, we worked like a family.”

Fear of failure

After that, I told my wife on the way home, "I feel really good about what I've done in the past."

'It is indeed a great thing to create a new business. It not only creates many jobs, but it affects many people's lives and further develops a greater nation.'

Creating a new business is one thing, but running a successful and long lasting company is another. When I worked as an employee in previous jobs, I had a fear of getting laid off with no savings when I had to support my family. There were always mortgages, car payments, insurance payments and more, in addition to day to day expenses.

When I hired employees, I felt responsible not to put their jobs at risk and had to make sure the company grew and was profitable. In the IT business, you could easily get caught up by new competition and be taken over with the introduction of new technology.

When I was running the business, I was unable to relax because of the 'fear of becoming a failure'. I had a habit of constantly thinking about the worst case scenario and I couldn't just sit around and wait for results. In order to prevent the occurrence of unexpected situations, I thought about all possible variables and prepared alternatives for worst case scenarios. At the same time, I made sure to avoid the same mistakes from repeating themselves. Some employees called me a micro manager and weren't comfortable with me taking care of the details, but I couldn't help it because of the 'fear of failure'.

Leading by example

As the size of the company grew, so did the amount of work to be done. Especially at the end of each quarter, the factory was in a frenzy trying to meet quarterly goals. Even though many employees worked more than 60 hours a week, we were always short-handed. When the delivery date was imminent, I worked at the assembly lines with vice presidents packing boxes. When it came to getting things done, there were no limits to responsibilities regardless of rank.

In the morning we brought donuts and bagels for the employees and also catered lunch and dinner. Later, as the numbers grew, we built them a cafeteria. This gave me a chance to eat with employees and have casual conversation with them. I tried to create working environments where all could work happily. I didn't run the company with authority, rather I tried to lead employees by example. I worked like a family with my employees.

Since I was poor during my childhood and couldn't afford any waste, I developed a habit of saving. So, I looked around every corner of the company to see if there were unnecessary lights turned on, faucets leaking, or if things that could still be used were thrown away. I also considered it unnecessary waste to use separate rooms just to sleep, so I even shared a room with employees while traveling on business trips. When I met with clients, I was persistently engaged in sales because I couldn't tolerate wasting time. While I was busy traveling frequently on business trips, I was still the first to work and remained until the end.

Relied on common sense

When I first started Fibermux, I had a lot of trials and errors because I didn't have any business experience besides managing product development and production. I had to face so many new things but I wasn't afraid to ask around and learned from experts. After gathering ideas from them, I had to make the decisions in the end. I thought I was a quick learner and had good common sense. After a while, I became a good problem solver.

Looking back, these competencies may have developed during my school days and my time in the military. Since I was a child, I had difficulty adapting to situations I didn't agree with, so I had to find a breakthrough. Instead of being forced to do something I didn't like to do, I did what I really wanted. Through this, I was able to gain various experiences and I was able to grow my creativity, improvisation and problem solving ability. Whenever I had a chance to talk to young people in a lecture, I asked,

"How can you feel a sense of accomplishment and presence while living if you are being dragged on without knowing your potential? Can life be happy without a sense of accomplishment and happiness?

Do not blindly waste your time. Find your favorite things and things that you can do well. Since I had a variety of experiences other than studying during my school days, I was able to discover my own potential and problem-solving skills. These capabilities have had a big impact on real business management."

Broadening understanding and judgment skills are very important regardless of the type of job, the nature of work, and the level of work. But can we learn these competencies through textbooks alone? Rather than fearing new things, taking on challenges can foster your growth.

DNA of a Korean

When I first came to America with the American Dream, few people knew about Korea. I was often asked,

"Are you Japanese or Chinese?"

"I'm from Korea."

"Korea? Are you from North or South?"

At that time, being asked these questions made me feel ashamed.

During those years, Korea was underdeveloped and Japan was far ahead in many fields. When I visited Japan in the 1980s, I was envious and wondered to myself, 'When will Korea become like Japan? Would it be possible in 50 years?' It was very clean and the people were very nice.

30 years later, a miracle happened in Korea. We became number one in shipbuilding. Samsung and LG replaced SONY,

Panasonic, and Hitachi's reputation in electronic devices. Samsung became one of the largest manufacturers in the world. There are only 7 countries that make automobiles and Hyundai became one of them. The recent accomplishments of my home country made me so proud and living in a foreign country made me even more patriotic to my homeland.

Through the 1988 Olympic Games in Seoul, the power of our people became known to the world. 10 years later in 1998, I saw Seri Park winning the LPGA and I was so thrilled I couldn't stop my tears. I was so excited that I even gave my daughter, who was born that year, her name. Seri Park's kids who have grown since then have also steadily remained at the top of the LPGA, surprising the world.

The determination to succeed that was unique to Korea earned the country the title "Miracle of the Han River," and my success was made possible by the DNA of Koreans flowing in me!

CHAPTER 4

Where Happiness Comes From

A life of splendor

My former Beverly Hills home

In 1999, I sold Xylan for $2 billion. As a result, hundreds of employees became millionaires and I also made a substantial amount of money. When I first moved to the U.S., I had only $2,000 in my hands. I worked day and night to earn money for a living and to pay for tuition, and I didn't have time to rest even on weekends. Finally, in 23 years, I achieved amazing results and was able to enjoy free time and financial leeway.

In hopes of doing things I had never done in the past, I bought a one-acre house in Beverly Hills for $15 million. It had a swimming pool, a tennis court, eight bedrooms and the house alone was over 14,000 square feet. The house was surrounded by tall walls and there was an expansive driveway leading to the grounds once you entered through the gate. The house was decorated with a beautiful French garden and it cost more than $100,000 a year to maintain the garden alone. It took two years to collect paintings to fill empty walls and I also hired a Russian artist to paint murals on the ceiling. I even received a sports car as a gift from a venture capital company who made a lot of money through me.

I also bought a big villa on the shore of Lake Arrowhead and purchased a yacht. When I was still working, I flew economy class in order to save money for the company. Now that I was living a comfortable life, I managed to take my family on lavish vacations around the world flying first-class. I enjoyed inviting guests to my home.

Everyone was happy when they were treated to the best food and wine in a beautifully decorated house and this made me proud and happy. Success allowed me to enjoy a more luxurious life than I had ever imagined while also gaining access to the high-class social culture of America.

One day, I had lunch with Dick Troop, a lawyer who was my long-time investor and a board member of Xylan.

"Steve, do you want to join me as a director of the LA Opera? We don't have any Asian directors but I think you deserve to be the first."

"What do you do when you become a director of the Opera?"

"You'll sponsor the opera and advise them on its operations. Merely having a lot of money doesn't make you eligible, but only socially respectable individuals can become a director. I'll recommend you if you would like and I'm sure the other directors will welcome you."

This was how I became the director of the LA Opera and to me, it was validation that I had become an honorable person. When you become a board member they expect you to donate about $50,000 a year in addition to purchasing gala concert and season tickets. Although I lived in the U.S. for a long time, there were very few occasions that I participated in social gatherings other than for business.

Soon after joining the board, I was contacted by the director of the board, Leslie Pam.

"Steve, I'm Leslie, your mentor and I want to welcome you as a director of the LA Opera and invite you and your wife to my home for dinner. It's a small gathering and I'm going to cook for you."

When we arrived at his house on the top of a Hollywood Hill, a beautiful opera melody floated through the air. I walked in thinking the audio sound was loud, but it turned out that the young tenor was actually singing in the living room. He said that he came from Italy to audition with Placido Domingo, who was then the musical director of the Los Angeles Opera. Before dinner was served, small concerts were prepared for the guests and it was very impressive. It was the first Salon concert I ever experienced and it was quite a cultural shock to me.

Salon concert

After that experience, I often organized salon concerts at my home. The parties had a formal dress code and typically there were around a hundred guests. I decorated the house with beautiful flowers, hired one of the best caterers in town, and prepared nice wines. When guests arrived, we had about 30 minutes of cocktail time, a concert for over an hour and then dinner.

I assembled a performance team with Korean musicians living in LA. By setting talented Korean musicians on stage, I wanted to leave a lasting impression to Americans who had few chances of encountering Korean artists. After the concert, guests were seated at their tables and served high quality food and wine. Everyone had a great time.

Many times, I held fundraising concerts for musicians who needed financial help to continue their musical studies. I paid all party expenses and each couple donated $300 for the musicians.

Whenever world-renowned sopranos like Sumi Jo, and Hyekyung Hong were visiting LA to perform in the LA Opera, I invited them to my home and held wonderful parties.

When I was busy with work, I had few opportunities to have access to classical music and I never imagined I would be supporting artists. Once I became the director of the LA Opera, I was able to attend many concerts and enjoy the opera to my heart's content.

During my time as the director, I learned that so many Koreans were majoring in classical music and I was surprised to find that more than 25 percent of the students at the famous Juilliard School of Music in New York were Koreans. There were also quite a few Koreans who have won the prestigious international competition for excellence.

'What can I do to help our young Korean musicians who display outstanding talent in the classical field?' Upon consideration, I established the Korea International Music Foundation (KIMF).

I became the chairman of the board and Hayeon Cho and Dr. David Lee, who would later become a real estate tycoon in LA, participated as directors. We raised $50,000 a year and gathered young Korean musicians from around the world to hold a competition at Colburn Theater in downtown. Musicians gathered from Seoul, New York and other parts of the U.S. and Europe. It became a valuable and meaningful time for everyone including those who provided homestays for overseas Koreans.

Salon concert performed by Korean musicians

Happiness comes from recognition

Those who donate more than $100,000 to UCLA, a university near Beverly Hills, are invited to a party organized by the President of the university.

One year, I was invited to the party because I donated $1 million to the UCLA Dental School. When I walked into the party, there were about 100 couples in fancy dresses and suits, but when I looked around my wife and I were the only Asians. Even so, no one recognized 'Steve Kim, the man of Xylan's success story,' as reported by major U.S. media at that time. Only a few days prior, I was a leading figure in the industry, but I remained a stranger to all the attendees who didn't recognize me.

I returned home with a feeling of solitude among a fancy crowd. I felt empty and I realized that being successful did not necessarily equate to being happy. I think a big part of the reason people pursue success is not only for money but also to receive recognition from others.

An uninvited visitor after success

After the success of Xylan and selling it at the peak of its success, I had enough money to do whatever I wanted without any time constraints. I even thought, 'This must be why people are trying to be successful and rich!' However, material pleasures didn't last very long.

When I had my first villa, I invited family and friends over so we can have fun fishing, boat riding, golfing and hiking together. But after a while, the novelty of it wore off and it was no longer fun and exciting. No matter how expensive it was, it didn't feel special and neither did the parties. When guests returned home, I felt lonely and empty. Many envied my life, but I struggled with emptiness and loneliness and I was afraid I would spend the rest of my life feeling this way.

When the cost of living each month was so tight, my dream was to be able to occasionally eat out with my family. When I was too busy running a business, I wished I had some personal time for pleasure and I wanted to travel from time to time. Looking back, I was much happier then.

An attempt to find new passion

There were people who encouraged me to start a new business, but I felt I had already accomplished more than enough and had no reason to go back to the competitive world. I wanted to find something that I could do with my experience rather than burdening myself with it.

Upon deliberation, I decided I wanted to become a venture capitalist. I was confident in selecting new startups and providing advice for the management to help companies grow. One day, I had a chance to have lunch with the President of Alcatel in Paris. I told him,

"I'm raising venture capital funds. I think I can do it well based on my past experience."

"Is that right? I was planning to invest in the U.S. What if Alcatel invests half of it?"

I raised $100 million and finally found a new passion by establishing Alcatel Ventures.

In the 1990s, many startups including Xylan were very successful, so many investors made big money. Consequently, there were too many start-ups and investors chasing them. When I started Alcatel Ventures in 2000, it was the beginning of the IT bubble. I found that it was very difficult to find promising start-ups and the valuation was ridiculously expensive. I tried very hard over a year to find a good investment but I decided to return the money to investors rather than taking the risk.

Soon after, I became a board member of Nara Bank in Koreatown. Banks seemed to be a relatively easy business, as they do not have to constantly develop and produce new products like the highly competitive IT industry. So, I thought of buying a small bank and operating it.

In 2002, I established a new financing company called New Commercial Capital. However, it didn't need my daily involvement when I recruited a president who was experienced in the field. As money and honor were given by big success, it seemed almost impossible to find a job that would bring me passion.

A permanent return after 30 years

While traveling around many places with my family, I stayed in Korea for about a month in August 2006. I wanted my children who were born in the U.S. to learn more about my homeland.

As I got off at the Incheon Airport, I could see clear skies and long roads in the distance. When I first left Korea, there were a lot of shabby buildings but just a few decades later, Seoul became like any other developed city with high skyscrapers and modern buildings. The country was very clean and people were very kind wherever we went.

Incheon International Airport achieved world's No. 1 in airport service for 12 consecutive years

We travelled to many famous mountains, islands, beaches and historic sites in Korea. We enjoyed beautiful scenery and delicious food. It was very interesting for the children to travel and it filled their curiosity about their parents' home country.

When I came home after the long trip with my family, I had a strange feeling as if my home was in Korea and I came here for vacation. My wife had a similar feeling and asked me, "What if we move back to Korea? It would help our children find their Korean identity and learn their mother tongue."

At first, I was shocked to hear her statement because I never thought about moving back to Korea. After some careful consideration, I thought that if I moved to Korea, I could focus more on the Dream Hope Future foundation, which was established in 2000. This was an opportunity to find something meaningful to do and regain my passion in life.

At the age of 27, I left Korea with only $2,000 in my hand and fear of settling in a foreign country. My dream was to become an engineer and have an ordinary life like many others. 30 years later after achieving great success, I returned to my homeland. While I was gone my country made huge strides and became a developed country. They called it the Miracle of the Han River because no other countries had ever achieved as much growth in such a short time.

Evening scenery in Seoul, Korea

CHAPTER 5

Meaningful Life in Korea

Steve Kim's Success story, 'Dream, Hope, Future' published

Lecture for Korean Military Academy

At first, it wasn't easy adapting to life back in Korea even though it's where I was born and raised. Seoul is a very crowded city with over 10 million people and everybody seemed to be very busy. The life style was much different from LA.

Then I happened to get to know a college professor. When he heard about my success story, he recommended that I publish a book.

"Mr. Kim, these days, our teenagers cannot find good Korean role models. The success you achieved will give valuable lessons and inspiration to our youth."

"I'm not good at writing and I never imagined I would write a book about myself."

"Mr. Kim, please don't just say no, consider it seriously. Someone could write it for you. It is important for you to share your experience and wisdom. Your accomplishment through strong will could ignite a challenging spirit for many people."

I thought my story could give courage and hope to the youth who had given up their dreams. In addition, my experience of trial and error could help those who were starting new businesses.

In September 2007, I published a book titled *Asia's Bill Gates, Steve Kim's Success story, Dream, Hope, Future* Upon its release in bookstores, the book caused a sensation beyond my expectations and requests for interviews and lectures poured in from various places.

KBS TV 'Do Dream Show'

I was invited to talk on many TV shows. In addition to appearing on TV, I was given many speech opportunities for a number of different audiences. I was very busy touring the country more than 200 times a year and when I was in the office, countless people came and sought my advice.

Newly discovered mission

After publishing my autobiography, I finally had passion in life by finding meaningful things to do. I had eagerly waited for my time and experience to be so precious! I was very proud to have successfully fulfilled my duties to my employees and investors, but I didn't know how rewarding it would be for my experiences to give courage, challenge and new hope to others.

When I was in the office, many people who had come across various problems such as difficulties in business, questions about startups, and personal problems, came and sought my advice. During the time that I was doing business, I was desperate for a mentor, so I offered my advice with the utmost sincerity to those who came to see me.

In the meantime, I received a lecture request from a high school principal outside of Seoul. When I entered the auditorium where more than 400 students were gathered, I was greatly shocked by the unexpected situation. I couldn't sense any anticipation or

curiosity for the lecture. The students just sat there disinterested and didn't listen to the lecture at all. It took me a lot of effort to get their attention.

Upon finishing the lecture and returning home, I wondered, 'why did the youth, who should be filled with curiosity, become like this?' I couldn't shake this thought from my head. Thereafter, I learned that the current educational environment of the youth was so different from when I left Korea 30 years ago.

When I was growing up, most families had many children and parents couldn't afford to care about their children's education. There were also very few students entering college because they were so poor. I had three sisters and one younger brother but I, as the eldest son, was the only one who was able to receive a college education. Nowadays, most families have only one or two children and parents are so obsessed with their children's education.

Because Korea is so competitive, most public enterprises, large corporations, civil servant organizations, and teaching institutions have an open recruitment system. This means that one must graduate from a good college with exceptional grades in order to have a chance at being hired. As a result, they have their eyes set on entry into the prestigious university in Seoul rather than their local colleges.

With such ambitious goals, kids' lives are centered on college entrance exams even before they start elementary school. Most of the children have become helpless, losing their pure curiosity and inquisitiveness while being blindly dragged along by their parents' expectations and greed, irrespective of their own will.

I couldn't just turn away from the youth who had no motivation or goals for their future ahead. After that experience,

I focused my lectures on the youth as my top priority. However, it wasn't easy capturing the focus of children who were exhausted by the entrance-exam focused education they were receiving.

I needed to try something different in order for them to open up their ears and pay attention to what I wanted to share. So, instead of a suit, I dressed in jeans and a T-shirt and approached them as a friendly uncle singing with them and showing them magic tricks. I shared my life story and talked about how it was possible to achieve my success after overcoming so many difficulties.

"Everyone was born to be happy. However, happiness isn't just given, you have to earn it. One must personally make their own happiness by thinking about it carefully.

First, you need to find out what you like and what you do well. You are at a sensitive age, so it is the best time to acquire new things. I want you to read a lot of books instead of purposeless study, and to discover yourself by engaging in many other activities like sports, arts, and after school club activities. Whatever you do, you have to have goals and objectives for your future.

Do you know how proud and happy you will be, once you immerse yourself in something? Every time you do well, your confidence and sense of achievement will grow tremendously."

It was difficult to keep the attention of these children for even 10 minutes. To maintain their focus during the lecture, I asked questions and gave my book as a prize to students who answered. These children who usually didn't listen to the words of others cheered and applauded when they were moved by the lecture. By capturing the focus of each student one by one and by working hard to convince them, two hours just flew by.

After the lecture, I let the students voluntarily come up to the stage and present what they learned and how they planned to apply it to their lives.

When young boys with broader shoulders than me poured their hearts out about troubles that were built up inside, my heart broke for them. How difficult must it be for these kids who all have different skills and interests to be forced down the same path? Why must it be so difficult for the youth who should be running so brightly and enthusiastically?

Before leaving, I signed the books that I gave and took pictures with the students. While escorting me out, a student commented, "Mr. Kim, I will definitely implement the lessons you taught us today. I will remember you for a very, very long time. Please don't forget me either."

It's hard to imagine speaking for two hours to hundreds of students who are not ready to listen. It was to the extent that every time I finished my lectures, my shirt would be soaked in sweat and I would have to change in my car on the way to the next school. The journey was difficult to the point that even I considered it a great challenge, but I did my best without neglecting my passion.

I wanted to share a couple of letters I received from students after the lecture:

"Hi Mr. Kim,

I was stifled by the same repetitive life every day. From dawn to night, I went to school and tutoring, but my study didn't fit my aptitude and it was not interesting. My parents and teachers didn't understand me and told me that in order to get a good job and live well, you have to study hard whether you like it or not.

But today, you told me to 'just cover your book when you really don't feel like studying and wander around until you find what you like to do.' My heart was beating! 'Oh, there are some people in this world who understand me!' The reason I've been so unhappy and unmotivated is because my life goal was decided by my parents, not by me.

From now on, I will seriously think about my life and lead the way. If I can do my best and be responsible for my actions, I think my parents will trust and support me.

Mr. Kim, today you enlightened me and gave me courage. I will surely be successful. Please don't forget me, thank you so much!"

"Hi Mr. Kim,

Do you remember the girl who cried and asked you to write 'Yes, you can do it!' when you signed the book for me after the lecture? I was deeply moved by you! These days I've been exhausted and I went into the auditorium without any expectation. But when I saw you wearing a leather jacket and jeans, I felt that you were different from other lecturers I had seen before. Even though we were meeting for the first time, you were very friendly and you showed us a lot of affection.

*When you listed the '***Seven Key Words of Success****: earnest goals, self-esteem, enthusiasm, confidence, favorability, habits, and communication skills,' I thought to myself, 'Wow!' I was suffocating and always uneasy because I felt like I was being chased by the college entrance exam. So, when you said we should find what our dreams are through various experiences, I couldn't help but tear up. Like you said, I will raise my self-esteem and endlessly pour my passion into a meaningful goal. Also with the confidence that I can do*

it, I will create good habits and try to become a person that gives favor to others.

I will apply everything you told me in today's lecture and I hope to become a person like you. You have become my role model. As I am writing this letter, I am looking at the frame that contains the paper you signed and the impression you left during the lecture keeps coming back to me. I felt again that your lecture gave me a lot of change and positive influence. I would like to say that I will definitely make my dream come true and that this lecture has become a turning point in my life. Thank you very much for giving such a wonderful lecture that changed the life of this one schoolgirl."

Children are happy just to have someone understand and sympathize with their situation. The time I spent giving hopes and dreams to these children, who have been driven to difficult educational circumstances by the greed of their parents, has become special and meaningful work for me.

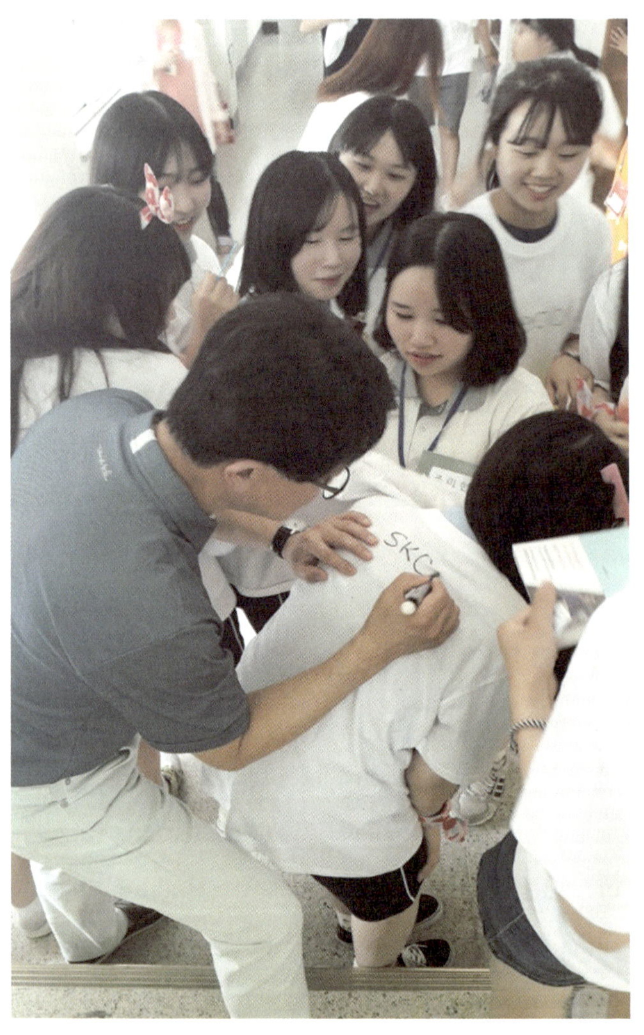
SKC

Third venture, DHF Leadership Center

When I stepped in the car leaving the children behind, a feeling of sadness came over me. I knew that they had to go back to their classrooms and continue with what they had been used to. As long as the educational environment didn't drastically change, I doubted they could make changes themselves.

'What is necessary for our youth to find breakthroughs and be happy?' After deep thought, I established the Dream Hope Future(DHF) Leadership Center in November 2009. I've never been involved in the education business, but I started my third venture with a mission and passion specifically for the youth.

The purpose of the new venture was not to make money but to give dreams and hopes to the youth. We had to come up with totally new methods of educating students. We created content for students to experience change and emotions through their voluntary participation.

The 'DHF leadership camp' consists of 16 hours in 2 days. Whenever schools want to host our camp, our instructors travel to the school wherever they are located. They arrive the day before to remove all the desks in the classroom and only the chairs are left.

The camp is programed to initiate self-awakening, to focus on finding and expressing one's true self, and to engage in their own voluntary participation. Instructors are not forced or injected unilaterally, but students, who we call leaders, voluntarily take part in every session by raising hands.

On the first day, our program begins with self-introduction in a creative way, followed by sharing accomplishments, a most

challenging experience, and vision for the future. One of the sessions is a time to speak up about wounds and trauma that have not been shared with others. People need a lot of courage to bring out stories that have been buried in their hearts and haven't ever been revealed to others. However, by shaking off deep wounds, they are able to receive comfort and encouragement from friends and instructors. Through this process, they realize that they are precious and are able to free themselves of grudge and anger.

It's not easy for leaders who have never presented in front of others to come out and speak. Therefore, the ability of the instructor is absolutely crucial to achieving results. It helps open the minds of the leaders if they can relate to instructors who grew up with hardship in a similar environment and overcame their adversity. In addition, the instructors can honestly share their life stories with the leaders, giving them concrete challenges and ways of changing to apply to their own lives.

While trying to find the best instructors for our program, we try to hire young people who have the right personality and a mission for the youth. After 3 months of extensive training, they become qualified as instructors. Two of the instructors become a team and head to schools for the leadership camps.

After long preparation, the first camp was held at Seoul Women's University. When the camp was over, I watched the graduation ceremony with the college officials unknowing what the results would be.

When it was time to share testimonies, a student immediately raised her hand and came to the front saying, "Sir, I got exactly what I needed through this program. Please make it so that every

Graduation ceremony after two-days camp

student in our school can get this education." After this student tearfully shared how this camp touched her life, one by one more students came forward and passionately shared how they were personally touched and what realizations they made.

All those who witnessed this event were blown away and the emotions I felt could not even be put into words. It was work that I had never done before and simply moved forward with because I felt saddened for them, but the results were unbelievable. As a result, I gained confidence in our content and gained assurance of this program.

Upon witnessing leaders change dramatically after hearing their stories, the instructors who share their shameful pasts and experiences of suffering, feel enormous achievement and reward. Therefore, the program becomes a meaningful learning experience for both the instructors and the leaders.

Since then, I started to worry about how to expand. It was very difficult to find the right person to grow the business. I was frustrated, but I had no one to share my anxieties with. In the meantime, I found a general manager who was experienced in youth education. Through her, the details of the business started to unravel and it has grown exponentially each year.

She oversaw the entire business and even took on marketing. She created the content, hired and trained young instructors who had no experience in lecturing, and visited the places where I lectured in the past to open the door for our camp. She drove all over the country with a stamina that was unbelievable for a woman of such small stature. She usually visited three to four places on each business trip. I was amazed with how she persuaded everybody with passion for our camp. She had a mission to devote herself to the youth and was a gift sent to me by God.

Miracle camp

I would like to introduce some examples of how our camp succeeded and what the results were in the field.

"Because I am very shy and introverted, I have never presented in front of the public. However, day by day I found myself more confident to raise my hand quicker and go up to the front even when it wasn't asked of me. Before that, I couldn't even imagine myself speaking in front of people. It's possible no one may believe me. I changed so much that even I can't believe it myself."

"I said things that I was never able to say to anyone in front of so many people that I don't even know. While sitting in an empty chair, I was unable to control the sudden tears that flowed out as soon as my name was called. After assuring myself, I felt relieved inside. From now on, I think I can love myself and have strength. To

be honest, I didn't expect that my friends who heard my story would understand me. However, they all hugged me and gave me comfort so I was very grateful. 'Dream Hope Future' is the best."

"Until now I didn't know why I had to live. I thought no one cared about me and wouldn't even notice if I died. It was so hard to continue living. However, I will never think that way moving forward. I learned that I am an important person and that I am not alone. Through 'DHF leadership camp', I found a reason why I need to continue living."

Leaders actively changed through voluntary participation

"Since I was young, I lived with my grandmother. So, when I saw my friends complaining about their parents I was speechless but was also jealous. I don't even know my parents' faces and my grandmother was very old so we couldn't communicate well with each other. I was very resentful of my irresponsible parents who gave birth to me and I felt like I was so unlucky in life.

However, after listening to a friend's story that was more difficult than mine, I was so grateful of my grandmother who always worried for me. Thank you for helping me change my perspective. I am lucky to have received this training. I hope all students in Korea will receive this training. Thank you very much."

Our instructors do not give up until the end to produce results. After witnessing so much change in these students, teachers and parents said, "This is a miracle. I never imagined that students who wouldn't ever do this no matter how much teachers pleaded, would voluntarily raise their hand and come to the front."

Before and After two-days camp

In fact, the person most surprised by these continuously had opportunities to share their stories and consequently grew more confident and gained fulfillment without even knowing it. After the two-day camp, it resulted in remarkable change and earned us the name 'Miracle Camp'. Teachers and parents who watched the completion ceremony, said that it was hard to believe.

"That child is normally not like that. I've been teaching the class for two years and I've never seen him talk to anyone. It's also the first time I've seen him smile so brightly. The fact that he's presenting up front

so sharply… how could something like this happen? It's unbelievable."

"What have you done with our kids? Every single student, without exception, is overflowing with confidence and has become extremely bright and pleasant in demeanor. Students who haven't been able to attend the camp have been coming to the office every day begging to attend."

When change in students became evident after training, word spread by mouth through the students' parents.

Graduation Ceremony after two-days camp

Most meaningful venture

With DHF instructors

The demand for our camp had grown rapidly and we had to recruit many instructors to support growth. There were more than 50 instructors, so more than 10 vans were needed to go to schools all over the country. To reduce the distance traveled by instructors to schools scattered across the country, two branches were established in central and southern Korea.

In 2014, more than 40,000 people received our education through 1,200 classes. The camp originally designed for the youth had been expanded to college students, teachers, parents, employees and military personnel. These results clearly show that our camp is necessary and meaningful for everyone.

One time, I went to the Second Military Support Command to give a lecture and concert to the soldiers. I brought along a pianist, violinist, cellist and soprano singer. When I introduced our camp to the general, he told me that soldiers desperately needed our program and asked us to educate more than 2,000 soldiers in the army base.

Lecture concert with piano trio and soprano

At that time, our manpower barely met the needs of the youth. However, the general manager who was sitting next to me came up with an idea.

"Commander, if you find a few soldiers who could be qualified as instructors, I will train them just like our instructors."

At the end of our discussion, 12 instructors were selected and received instructor training by the general manager for three months. The trained instructors carried out the camps within the unit and had remarkable results.

Suddenly, I wanted to expand this program to the whole army. I became acquaintances with Junkyu Chang, the Chief of the Army through the many lectures and concerts we delivered to military bases. I paid him a visit to the Army headquarter and said,

"General, as you have probably heard the 2nd Army base adapted our program and had amazing results. I am convinced that our program is a must for the entire military. What if I provide support to expand the program throughout the entire army base?"

"Mr. Kim, it would be greatly appreciated if you could do that! In fact, I was struggling with 'elite military officers' and establishing soldiers' 'integrity.' Due to the rigid military culture, soldiers with inner troubles can't share with colleagues or bosses that they are suffering. I would be so grateful if DHF leadership camp could be introduced throughout the military."

During the six months following the meeting with the general, we piloted the 'Military Leadership Camp' for 4,300 soldiers of 42 divisions, and many commanders attended the completion ceremonies and witnessed the results.

On January 11th, 2017, our DHF Foundation and the Korean Army Headquarters signed a contract to expand this program to

Business agreement ceremony in the army headquarters

Training at our company to serve as an army instructor

all the army bases. We have trained a number of instructors who applied from many different army bases. Currently, 50 instructors that we trained are conducting our program as an instructor in each unit. We plan to increase the number to 100 in the next year. I will continue to support this meaningful project and I believe this is the path to patriotism.

The DHF Leadership Center was established to save the youth who were suffering from the current education system. I also wanted to give good jobs to young people by hiring them as instructors. While most other education companies hired part-timers or freelance instructors, I hired young people as full-time employees who never had any experience as instructors but who were full of empathy and sense of duty for the disheartened youth. By providing them with a happy workplace, we are able to deliver the 'Miracle Camp' and the instructors are called 'Miracle Makers' in the field. I have been spending about $1.3 million every year for the leadership camp alone, but this has been the most meaningful and valuable thing I've ever done.

DHF Leadership Center employee workshop

CHAPTER 6

Noblesse Oblige

Most precious use of money

Annual DHF Scholarship Camp in Seoul

When I came to Korea, people wondered how wealthy I was and how much I would pass on to my children. What I want to leave behind for our children is not a lot of wealth, but a way to live happily with sincerity in the right spirit. I think it is more important to pass on good character and good habits as long as I provide them with the basis for living comfortably.

The legacy I received from my parents was 'poverty', 'a loving heart', and the 'hungry spirit'. Poverty became the driving force for my success. I had a strong will for a better life and I was driven by that.

Any parent would want their children to live a happy life. In order to do so, you should help them build a sense of accomplishment through their own efforts, because that will become a source of their happiness. When you feel that something is scarce, you have the desire to fill it and you can exert your passion to achieve it.

If children inherit all of their parents' property, their chance of achieving their own happiness is taken away. Moreover, it is common for a child who has inherited property without his or her own efforts to learn the value of money inappropriately. In other words, monetary legacies can become rather poisonous.

I believe it is right for the wealthy to fulfill their social responsibilities by practicing Noblesse Oblige in order to be respected by others. Annual charitable funds in the United States reach hundreds of billions of dollars, which include significant donations from people of all social standings. The important thing is not the amount of the donation but rather the heart and desire to help others. Many believe we have the strongest nation due to the greatness of ordinary people.

Family foundations are established so that hard-earned wealth can be used in society. After the foundations are established, funds are managed to be used towards meaningful projects. The Rockefeller Foundation, the Carnegie Foundation, and the Bill & Melinda Gates Foundation, are typical examples.

As a resident of the United States, where it was common to establish a family foundation and return some of your earnings to society, I founded the Steve Kim Foundation in 1997.

Simultaneously, I was supporting projects in China, North Korea, Bangladesh and Nepal. Then in 2001, I established the Dream Hope Future (DHF) Foundation in Korea. The foundation's goal was to help teenagers who had to give up their studies due to financial difficulties.

The foundation looks for students who are personable and competent but can't afford the tuition. Once they are chosen as scholarship students for the DHF Foundation, they are provided with scholarship funds until they graduate college. Upon graduation, the foundation helps them find good jobs so they can support themselves and help their family escape from poverty. Since the foundation was first established in 2001, it has helped many young people grow up to become great exemplary adults.

Following is a letter I recently received from a past scholarship recipient.

"Mr. Kim, I don't think you remember me, but my name is Hyojung Kim, a DHF scholarship recipient

Scholarship Camp for North Korean Youth

for five years from my senior year in high school until I graduated Handong University last year. I heard you are currently living in the U.S. and I'm sure that you are doing well.

I recently got a job at a nonprofit organization in Pohang as an administrator. My mother suggested that I spend my first salary in a way that is most meaningful to me. DHF Foundation is a very special place for me because I couldn't enter into the college without its financial support. Without the support of the Foundation, I can't imagine where I would be today. The help I received is incomparable to my donation, but I am grateful and would like to give back my first salary to the Foundation.

Thank you very much and I love you, Mr. Kim. Always stay healthy."

- DHF scholarship student, Hyojung Kim

I started my scholarship program in 2001 and have continued the work to date. Through this, hundreds of students have finished their studies and entered into the workforce.

We are still trying to expand the reach of the foundation by finding a place that is in desperate need of financial help. When boys and girls who've lost their parents, have to enter into society at the age of 18, it's likely they may face many difficulties along the way.

There are also many multicultural families from poor countries and many of their children may face similar problems. Hence, we are trying to expand the scope of our foundation to provide guidance along with financial support.

Scholarship for Yanbian

Apartment complex in Yanbian, China

In 2001, I went to Beijing before visiting Pyongyang in North Korea. When I arrived there, I found that my Visa to North Korea wasn't ready and had to wait a few more days. So, I decided to visit Yanbian located north of North Korea.

Over 1 million Korean-Chinese were living there and they had Korean speaking schools. They were immigrants from Korea in the early 1900s when Korea became a colony of Japan. They were very poor and they earned less than $1,000 a year, which mostly came from farming income. It was almost impossible for their children to attend college because tuition alone could cost $1,000 per year.

I thought, "Money could be spent more usefully here than in Korea. These people have the same blood as ours." In 2002, I set up on office and hired a few employees within Yanbian University of Science and Technology (YUST) and started the same scholarship program as in Korea.

Each year, foundation employees left their home and made visits across China to children in remote villages. These children, once selected as DHF scholarship recipients, became our family members.

Twice a year, we held camps at YUST. More than 400 scholarship students came from all over the country to attend the four-days camp. For some students, it took more than 20 hours to get to the summer camp because the transportation infrastructure was very poor. I asked,

"Wasn't it hard to travel for that long?"

"I've been waiting a year to join this summer camp. Compared to waiting, this is nothing."

These children seldom had the chance to leave their small village. I felt sympathy for them and I couldn't stop thinking about what more I could do for them. I tried to participate in the camp whenever possible and tried to inspire these children with stories of my early childhood. I shared with them how I overcame poverty to become who I was today.

Summer scholarship camp in Yanbian, China

A few years ago, the Chinese government took over YUST and didn't allow the missionary activity within schools. They also disbanded the operation of DHF foundation in China. It was quite painful to close the office that I had put so much work into for 15 years, and even more disheartening to lose connection with hundreds of scholarship students who were in desperate need.

A heartbreaking land, North Korea

When I was living in LA, I met Dr. Piljoo Kim, an expert on seed development. She was sending seeds to North Korea to help them solve the problem of food shortages. I was intrigued and expressed my willingness to participate in her cause, so I visited North Korea with her three times.

When I first arrived in North Korea, I was really shocked. It was much colder than I had thought and all the mountains were cleared of trees because they were used as firewood. When I followed Dr. Kim to a school just outside of Pyongyang, all the children were small and thin and shivered in summer clothes.

"What do you think of buying winter clothes for them before it gets colder? How many children are there in this town?"

"That's a great idea. There may be around 5,000 kids here."

I bought 5,000 pieces of underwear, coats and shoes from China and sent it to them in a hurry. I then met a Korean-American who was residing in Domun near Rajin, located to the

north of North Korea. He ran a small bread factory to feed the hungry people of Rajin, so I helped him expand his bread factory.

I also helped him build a fertilizer plant for farmers to increase their yields and helped the fishermen repair their old boats so they could continue fishing. Moreover, I found that there were no paved roads that connected the Chinese border to Rajin, so many North Koreans had to walk for hours on foot. After seeing that, I thought to myself 'how nice would it be if I could provide them with buses.'

In 2006, I bought 8 buses from China and sent them to Rajin. After six months of consulting with North Korean authorities, buses were running and small barter markets were created at the bus stops.

Before my return home, I set up a bread factory inside Pyongyang University of Science and Technology (PUST) that was founded by the YUST president. Thereafter, I sent the factory $50,000 a year to make 2,000 loaves of bread a day for their students

Nepal, the library closest to the sky

In 2008, to participate in the opening ceremony of the library funded by our foundation, I went to Nepal's Goli village with my wife, three young children, and Hangi Shim, the director of an organization called Poom.

Goli is located near Mt. Everest and sits 2,700 meters high above the ground. To get to Goli, it takes 10 hours on bus from the capital of Nepal and another day of trekking on foot.

I flew to Goli by helicopter with my children. The ceremony was held in the traditional manner of the Serpa people. The welcoming ceremony prepared by the villagers and children still moves my heart and remains vivid in my memory until this day. We will never forget the night we camped under the millions of stars pouring overhead.

Oh, Bangladesh!

In 2011, I happened to read a book called 'Mission'. It was a testimony of Pastor Park, a missionary of 20 years in Bangladesh. The book described the pastor's missionary work while risking his life. I was moved by his book and met him thinking I could do something for the people of Bangladesh, one of the poorest countries in the world.

That summer, I set up a bread factory and started making a few thousand loaves of bread every day to feed children in the Sunday schools at the churches he set up in the past. The bread, named

'Steve Rutier (in Bengali)', was rich in milk, butter and eggs. Hundreds of people, including children who came for prayer each night, filled their hunger with the bread we made.

In January 2012, when I first visited Dhaka, the capital city of Bangladesh, the city was saturated, messy, and in disarray. The people there organized a few welcoming ceremonies for me at the church and hundreds of residents flocked over, making it impossible to leave or enter.

Through the years I've seen many children in poor countries such as North Korea, Philippines, and Cambodia, but the children here looked very friendly and watched me with curios eyes.

Seeing them reminded me of growing up poor after the Korean War. At that time, the hungry children were fed with goods supplied by foreign missionaries and were able to receive education at the schools they founded. Thanks to their help, Korea was able to escape from poverty and destitution. I imagined the Bangladesh I was seeing could not be much different from Korea at that time. Having gone through that experience myself,

I felt empathetic for the children who couldn't eat or go to school due to poverty.

When I came back to Korea, I decided to set up a few schools and fully support the operation. In January 2013, we founded schools in three places with Pastor Park: Nolbok, Utdolkhan and Joythatpple. We also decided to manage the Molitech school and Tongi senior center, which were on the verge of shutting down due to financial difficulty.

Visiting Bangladesh with my daughter, Elizabeth

That spring, I visited Bangladesh again to attend the opening ceremony of the new schools where hundreds of local residents gathered in the school yard.

"I'm Steve Kim from Korea. When I was young, Korea was a very poor country like Bangladesh today. Like you, I lived in a room with seven family members. We were so poor and we couldn't eat properly. My mother taught me, 'The only way of getting over poverty is to study.' I studied really hard and went to the U.S. to study more.

I went to America because I wanted to live a better life. When I first arrived there I worked during the day and went to school at night. Later on I started my own business, but whenever I faced difficulties I prayed to God for help. Finally, through the love of God, I overcame adversity and became very rich.

You might ask why I am here. You and I look different and speak different languages, but we are brothers in God. God blessed me and he wanted to share his blessings with you."

I rallied ten times for four nights and five days and set up schools in six places, all while reflecting on myself and the work I was doing. I was grateful to God for allowing me to do these things.

When a new school is established in a certain area, hundreds of children who have been neglected get to wear pretty school uniforms, receive education, and also learn to praise God every Sunday. In total, more than 1,500 students studied at six Steve Kim mission schools and more than 500 students gathered at Sunday schools every week.

Not only did we pay for tuition, we also provided school uniforms, textbooks, school supplies, and sanitary supplies such as soap and toothpaste. Further, many jobs were created, including positions for teachers, administrative staff, and bread factory workers.

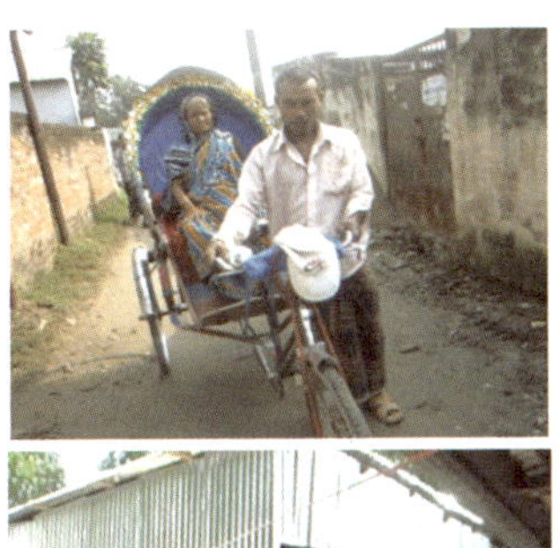

We distributed rice to residents, bought sewing machines for those who could physically work, and provided funds to start a business so they could become economically independent by opening a market.

Every time I visited there, I was filled with anticipation that there would someday be a leading figure in Bangladesh amongst the children who were part of the Steve Kim mission school.

CHAPTER 7

Return to the Land of Opportunity

An endless challenge

When I returned to my homeland in 2007 after 30 years of American life, I became so used to the lifestyle in Korea that I never thought about going back to America.

During my ten year stay in Korea, I was very busy giving over 100 lectures a year all around the country. The DHF Foundation also became involved in more meaningful projects, allowing us to expand our reach to others who needed our help. The demand for the leadership camp continued to grow and it was running well without my intervention. Moreover, touring the country giving lectures had also become less exciting over the years.

As I was wondering, 'what things make me excited?' I got a call from my friend Dr. David Lee in Los Angeles. He was originally a physician but now runs Jamison Property, one of the largest real estate developers in Los Angeles. I met him in 2000 and my family and I benefited a lot because we invested in many of his building projects. Robinson Ranch Golf, which I invested in with him way back in 2005, continued to run a deficit because of several years of extreme drought.

In 2016, he told me that he wanted to sell it if he found the right buyer. It was heartbreaking to hear that the beautiful 36-hole golf course was for sale. Suddenly, I thought it would be a meaningful project if I could take over and revamp it after being neglected for such a long time. After I told him my intent, I flew to Los Angeles the next day.

The golf course was simply ruined by years of drought. The reservoir, which supplied water to the golf course, was almost exhausted and the amount of water that could be purchased from the City was limited.

The 36-hole golf course consisted of an18-hole Valley course and an 18-hole Mountain course. The golf population had fallen sharply over the last decade and many golfers had left because of the extreme drought. So, I decided to close the Mountain 18-hole and concentrated on the Valley 18-hole. I stopped watering in

Golf course devastated by severe drought

front of the tee boxes where the ball couldn't reach, which saved almost 60 percent of the water that was originally being used. I hired a new general manager before I went back to Korea. After that, the golf course began to slowly recover.

Then, in July, a Sand Canyon fire occurred right next to our golf course. It was a big fire but fortunately, it only scarred a few holes and there was no major damage to the clubhouse. Seeing the charred mountaintops and black branches filling one side of the course, I was in despair.

The golf course had to be shut down for quite a while to repair the damage. So, I thought this could be an opportunity to remodel the golf course to a desert course and remodel the clubhouse.

A desert course is a desert-like golf course where DG (granite sand) is used instead of grass to the cover ground where the golf ball hardly drops. This would allow us to save as much water as possible.

To execute my idea, I hired a company that professionally remodels golf courses. Even when I was in Korea, I checked the status of the construction daily through the general manager. However, what I learned was that progress was much slower than the schedule and I couldn't understand exactly why.

I went back to the U.S. to find out what was going on and found that the general contractor was busy making excuses. So, I hired a new grading company and decided to overlook the construction myself. I bought a condominium in Koreatown, Los Angeles and went to the golf course every day.

While we were making some progress, there was a sudden flood in the middle of the drought. The heavy rain poured down huge piles of soil from the mountain around the golf course. The broken branches and ashes from the landslide blocked the water flow and all the newly planted grass was destroyed with muddy water. Three consecutive landslides delayed construction for months, and it was heartbreaking.

After acquiring the golf course, we suffered from all three major natural disasters including drought, fire and landslides. But after so much rain, the dry reservoir was filled and there was no longer any need to worry about water in the near future. What started out as heartbreak turned out to be a blessing for me!

Trial and error

I thought the desert course was a good alternative to save water and decided to remodel like the golf courses in Arizona, but it was a lot more complicated than I imagined.

It took a long time to cut the grass on the edge of the golf course and to fill it with the DG. I also found the fairway became narrower, which made it harder for golfers to play. I had to re-widen it by planting one million square feet of new sod, which cost me $500,000. The bigger problem, however, was that the grass I bought took a long time to

Too much grass cut while trying to conserve water

take root and turned yellow, rather than staying green. Every time I looked around the course, I told myself 'I should've left it alone and never tried to convert it to a desert course.'

Our golf course was originally designed by Ted Robinson, a famous golf course designer. The course had a reputation of beauty and was a very difficult course to play. The courses were very long and narrow and players were losing too many balls. While the course was being remodeled, three new tee boxes were built closer to the greens for easier play and stone walls were put up around the lakes in the golf course to stop the ball from the flowing into the water.

Remodeled lake with stone walls

Sand Canyon Country Club

Even though it was inevitable that it would take time to rebuild the golf course, I had to remodel the clubhouse in a hurry to reopen for already scheduled events. The paint was redone and the curtains, carpets and furniture were replaced. At the end of that year, I invited all the local residents to the clubhouse and shared food and wine with them. Many people approached me and said,

"I've been worried that the golf course would be left in ruins after the fires and mudslides. I have to tell you how happy I am to see everybody working hard day and night to restore the course."

"Thank you for inviting us to such a nice party at the beautifully remodeled club house."

I renamed 'Robinson Ranch Golf Club' to 'Sand Canyon Country Club' and wanted to give pride to the residents. After hearing some complaints from neighbors, I decided to open the restaurant every day except for evenings when we had banquets.

I hired an executive chef, Walter Kiczek, and he developed a new menu to serve a variety of foods. I organized special dinner events from time to time including Karaoke and dancing. However, since we are located away from the busy city, Valencia, there were many days that we had only a few guests. After many months had gone by, I had to cut down restaurant hours to minimize operating loss.

Rafael and his fellow workers

Residents overlooking the Desert course

The golf course reopened in March 2017 after 9 months of renovation. The 18-hole Valley course was renamed to 9-hole Valleys and 9–hole Desert courses. Residents overlooking the Desert course were the first to rejoice and the golfers who waited for the course to reopen showed gratitude.

Since we had enough water, I thought we better open another 9 holes and make a 27-hole golf course. It would be easier to maintain and we could accommodate big tournaments. Best of all, if I reopened 9 holes of the Mountain course, it would make the residents looking down, very happy.

I discussed the additional 9-hole construction with my general manager. He said he had to plant new lawns after overturning the ground because it was left with no water for over a year. He might have been right, but I wanted to get confirmation from the experts first.

Then, he introduced me to Rafael Cano, who was the superintendent at another golf course in Riverside. When I showed him the Mountain course, he took a closer look and said,

"If you manage well with water and fertilizer, the grass will grow back within 3 months because the roots are still alive."

"Are you sure?"

"I am sure, Mr. Kim. I managed three different golf courses over 20 years and I know what I am doing."

Working with Rafael

"Can you start right away? I will rent you an apartment close by."

He immediately moved in with his wife and three sons, and began working. I was stumped all day and watched what he did. Then miraculously, the grass began to come alive. It was great luck for me to meet him.

Rafael led his team to overhaul the golf course from early in the morning. 300,000 acres of golf course began to change shape and was covered by DG and mulch. We started to decorate the course with many trees and plants. In order to protect the grass on the fairway, we made an entrance with artificial turf where golf carts frequently passed.

Both Rafael and his crew moved in unison and had to do a lot of work. To motivate them and show my gratitude, I gave them free lunch and drinks every day in the snack bar. Nowadays, everyone visiting the golf course praises our fairways and green conditions.

Reborn Mountain course 2nd hole

New home for Rafael

One weekend, I saw Rafael's family picking up trash and repairing the grass on the golf course. I never asked them to, but they volunteered to take on this extra work. I was deeply moved by their actions and felt extremely grateful to them.

There were fairly sizable spaces in the maintenance building, which was used as the break room for maintenance crews. So, I decided to convert it into a new home for Rafael. Just like when I remodeled my own home, my wife and I poured a lot of attention into designing the floor plan, the interior, and picking furniture. It is scheduled to be completed by this fall and it will become a happy home for Rafael's family.

The reason I bought the golf course was not to make more money, but to spend my time and money in a meaningful way. Once I started a business, I wanted to prove to myself that I could do it by putting my best efforts forward.

The priority was to reduce losses as much as possible from the deficit accumulated over the years. To achieve that, I had to spend time elaborating with high-conscious employees about increasing efficiency and reducing waste. I also had to let go of lazy and dishonest people. While I was losing money, I had to invest millions of dollars on new golf carts, solar panels, artificial turf in the driving range, and replacing all the old maintenance equipment.

After all these efforts, the golf course started to generate a small profit.

A beautifully reborn golf course

In recent years, we had more rainfall than usual. The rainfall brought fresh shoots to the trees and wild flowers and sages of all kinds filled the mountain ridge. The oak trees, which were black as if they had died in the middle of the course, were also immeasurably rich with newly-grown leaves. It is simply remarkable to see brilliant flowers blooming on this vast land.

Oak tree resurrects after the fire

The golf course was reborn in just two years. The grass on the fairway was so thick that it was as soft as stepping on a rug. The rough around the green grew in thick and the greens were in perfect condition, not to be envious of any PGA course.

On the weekends, I play golf with my wife, my younger brother, and my sister-in-law. While we play, we're busy picking up litter, filling up divots, and repairing ball marks. Whenever I find something that needs Rafael's attention, I call him or send him pictures.

I've visited many famous golf courses, but it's difficult to come across many courses as beautiful as Sand Canyon Country Club, that is surrounded by the beautiful San Gabriel Mountains and an abundance of oak trees.

God looked at us with care and gave us new life. I believe that it is a life of gratitude for the grace of God that we managed to miraculously restore the beautiful nature of the course for many people to enjoy.

CHAPTER 8

Last Wishful Venture

Sand Canyon Resort

Sand Canyon Country Club in Santa Clarita, CA

When we were preparing for the opening of Mountain 9-hole, we had a neighbor helping us voluntarily. Dale Melson, who lives at the Robinson Ranch right next to the golf course, got out at dawn and cut the dead trees with hand-saws. Thanks to his interest and support, he became a close friend. One day, Dale asked me,

"Steve, do you have any special plans for the remaining 9 holes?"

"Well, I haven't thought about it yet."

"How about building a hotel here? When I have visitors from outside, there are no places to stay nearby so they have to go to Valencia, which is not close from here. "

Through conversation with him, I thought about developing a resort. When I lived in Los Angeles for many years, I often times wanted to get away with my children for long weekends or vacations but there were no resorts in Los Angeles County. The closest resort is Ojai Valley Inn, but it's still about 75 miles away from LA. When I tried to make a reservation with short notice, it was always full. With no options nearby, I had to travel to distant areas such as Palm Springs, San Diego, Santa Barbara or Hawaii.

Terranea resort in Palos Verdes opened about 10 years ago and is still the only easily accessible resort from Los Angeles. I thought if I built a nice resort in Sand Canyon, it would be great news for many people living in Los Angeles County. We will be much closer than Ojai Valley Inn and the surrounding landscape is ideal for a tranquil get away for families from everyday life, full of hustle and bustle of the city.

I was so excited about the new challenge that I wanted to get started right away. I visited Ojai Valley Inn with my wife to look around the lobby, banquet facilities, restaurants and spas. I met with the general manager and asked many questions about the facility and the operation. The next day, we headed straight to Terranea Resort in Palos Verdes. There, we also looked around the facilities and met with the marketing vice president to learn about their business. After benchmarking these two places, I was confident that I could build a superior resort.

I began to search for an architect who could undertake the project and was introduced to Magdalena Glen-Schieneman. She designed many Beverly Hills homes in the past 20 years and she was a person with creative artistry and pure passion.

My wife and I revisited both resorts with Magdelana and began to brainstorm how to design the best resort in Southern California. Soon after, we hired Ron, who works as a partner in a big architect company and has a lot of experience in resort design.

Resorts with the best views

Sand Canyon Resort & Spa site map

In the early stages of our work, one of the most important things we considered was how customers could have the best experience when they visited our resort. With a mere 40minute drive from Los Angeles, visitors will be able to see spectacular scenery and to relax amidst serene mountains vistas.

The 36-hole golf course and a housing complex was developed in Sand Canyon more than 20 years ago by a famous golf course designer, Ted Robinson. Over 400 acres of lush oak trees and 75 beautiful houses overlooking the golf course are surrounded by the San Gabriel Mountains.

Once the resort is built on the 75 acres of land, guests can enjoy the surrounding 27-hole beautiful golf course views and vistas of the Sierra Highway. There will be 360 degree views from the hotel resort as the buildings were oriented on site to facilitate visual relationship with surrounding nature.

For this resort to blend seamlessly with the beautiful landscape and neighboring houses, we tried to keep the height of the hotel building as low as possible. The resort's highest point is measured

33 feet from the ground of adjacent Robinson Ranch Road. The two-story villa is also designed to be less than 20 feet tall so as not to interfere with the views from inside the hotel.

We positioned the villas on the terraces cascading down toward the Robinson Ranch Road to further open the view corridors toward the surrounding mountains and existing oak groves.

In addition, all the rooms have balconies so guests can breathe fresh air when staying at the hotel. The hotel rooms, restaurants, spas and swimming pools were designed for guests to enjoy natural light and unique scenery.

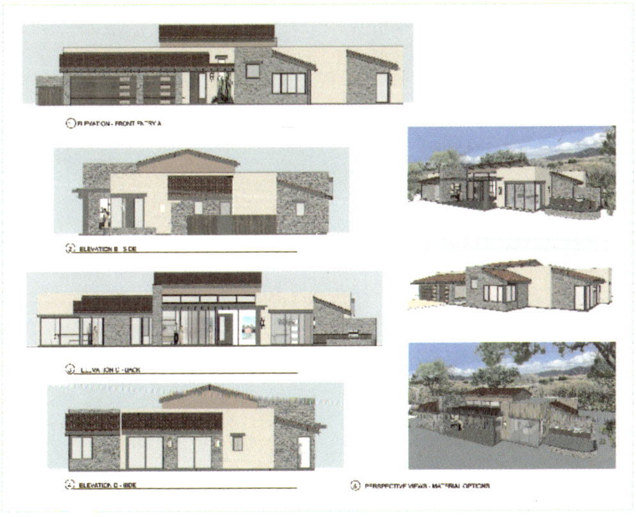

Single story Oak villa

The resort's best feature, natural landscape, is supplemented in most years by amazing wildflower blooms of many colors. Thanks to the sufficient rain we had for the past three years, flowers that have not been seen before have flourished in abundance and splendor.

Two story View villas

We are preserving a significant portion of the resort as native landscape to maintain the spectacular natural blooms and super blooms occurring here.

What's even more surprising is that sage bushes have sprouted new growth in all its green silver glory, and are coming up from the burned hills previously ravished by the recent fire. The appearance of the oak trees filled with green leaves that were once lit by the fire, feels like a miracle.

I have traveled to many famous resorts, but this place has such an extraordinary natural beauty that it's difficult to describe with words, but tranquility, serenity, peace and joy come to mind. The concept of the resort's landscape was created in harmony with the existing oak trees and native vegetation surrounding the course.

Canyon Country was the home of Indian tribes. Its urbanized phase began to develop after gold was discovered here and the first gold mine was established in the area.

"As the story goes, it was on a spring day in 1842 that mineralogist Francisco Lopez decided to take a leisurely nap beneath the tree now known as the Oak of the Golden Dream. While sleeping, Lopez had visions of being floated along a river of pure gold.

When he awoke, he found that he was famished and dug up some wild onions, but discovered flecks of gold (whole nuggets according to some accounts) clinging to the roots when he pulled the vegetables from the ground. All visions aside, this was the first documented discovery of gold in the California region.

After Lopez brought his gold to Los Angeles to be appraised, other prospectors began to smell the possibility of riches in the Western soil and the famous California Gold Rush was underway."

(Fragment from Atlas Obscura by Michael Bailey)

We worked to reflect the Californian rustic architectural style that has been the tradition and history of this area in our resort.

'Rustic Californian' architectural style is the mixture of the architectural elements found in mission revival, arts & crafts, and ranch styles. The elements from these architectural styles along the natural materials such as stone veneer, exposed fire resistive timbers, and clay tile roofs were used to create tranquil and consistent resort architecture.

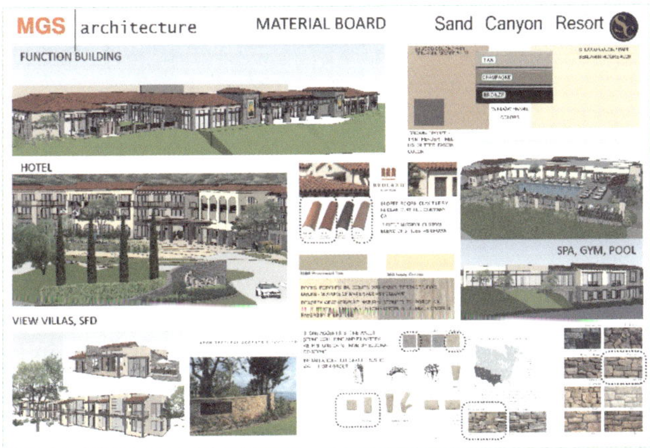

Material board

Resorts of the highest quality

Many, many times I wondered, 'How can I make the best resort in Southern California?' Whenever my wife and I had a chance, we visited some of the more popular golf resorts such as Pelican Hill, Pebble Beach, Aviara and Lacosta in San Diego.

No matter which resort we stayed in, we checked the size, height, and finish of the room. We even carefully touched the mattress, bedding, and bathroom towels. In addition, we carried a laser measuring instrument and observed everything including ceiling height, copper wire, flooring, the lobby, dining room, and ballroom. Unlike our previous trips, we were now interested in all aspects of the resorts, and all the good things have been applied to our project.

I wanted to decorate the lobby and rooms nicely so that as soon as guests entered the resort, they would be wowed by the hotel facilities. To make the guests feel comfortable during their stay, the size of the room was made spacious and the height of the ceiling was raised to over 9 feet. The bathroom is luxuriously decorated with a freestanding bathtub, an intelligent toilet and

Oak community villa

View villas

double sinks with ample countertop space. Each hotel room also has a generous balcony or terrace space.

Another aspect of a relaxed hotel resort stay revolves around dining. I wondered, how can hotel guests enjoy their meal without getting tired of the food? Originally, I planned to have three restaurants: a family restaurant, an Italian restaurant, and an Asian restaurant.

However, after I went on a business trip to Guangzhou, China a couple of months ago, I changed my mind. During my visit there, I stayed at the Sofitel hotel for over a week and had breakfast every morning at the same restaurant. I usually get tired of eating the same food more than once or twice but for some reason the food there never bored me.

I noticed that not only breakfast but also lunch and dinner were served as buffets at the restaurant. In order to observe how it ran all day, we tried breakfast, lunch and dinner on the last day of our stay. I saw that they had four different open kitchens and each of them served a different variety of food- seafood, meat, Asian, and baked goods and desserts.

When we came back, we decided to change the Family and Asian restaurant into a three meals buffet restaurant and keep the Italian restaurant as originally planned. This way, the local residents along with hotel guests could enjoy a variety of foods anytime.

We also carefully designed the size and location of the kitchen based on the passage of the service and the movement of employees. Since the location and size cannot be easily changed after the building is completed, all possibilities must be predicted and reflected in the design stage.

Most resorts have facilities for guests such as fitness, yoga, spa and beauty salon. We benchmarked Ojai Valley Inn, which has 23 treatment rooms in the spa. We designed our spas similar to the Ojai Spa with some changes.

Spa, Fitness Center, and Swinning pool

Spa building 1st floor　　Spa building basement

We added more specialized treatment rooms, a hot & cold sauna, mud room, salt room and scrub massage. We named it Golden Oak Spa to pay homage to Golden California Iconography and hope it will become the most sought after spa facility in Southern California.

Large corporations that have many offices around the US often use resorts for company retreats. Often, a few hundred people visit at the same time. To accommodate this number of guests, you have to have enough guest rooms, large ball rooms and sufficient meeting rooms. With that in mind, we originally planned for two ballrooms, one 7,000 sf and the other 2,300 sf. About a year and a half ago, when I explained the resort plan to the formal Mayor Lauren West of the city of Santa Clarita, she said,

"Steve, it's a great plan, but can you combine two ballrooms and make one big one? Santa Clarita is the 3rd largest city in Los Angeles County and it is growing very fast but we don't have large enough ballrooms to hold big events. The Hyatt hotel is the largest one in the city but it's only 4,000sf. So whenever we have a big event, we have to go to Universal city."

Restaurant & function building

"Is that right? This is a serious issue. Let me see if I could increase the size of the ballroom!"

Later on I increased the large ballroom to 10,000sf such that over 500 people can have dinner in comfort.

Family friendly resort

Unlike our childhood free of smart devices, it is unfortunate to see children spending so much time on smartphones and not engaged in outdoor play and family activities. I wanted to create a family-friendly resort because I wanted to minimize screen time for all children who stay here with their parents. To do that, we gathered ideas that could inspire their curiosity and materialized it with future offerings of a variety of amenities including classes, workshops and outdoor activities.

In addition to the adult pool, we plan to have a kid's pool, kid's arcade, kid's playground, miniature par 3 golf course, and tennis and pickle ball courts. We are also planning to open cooking and art classes for the children including drawing, painting, ceramics, collage, jewelry making and scientific fun with educational experiments.

Canyon Country is very popular with equestrians so there are a lot of horse ranches and miles of horseback riding trails in the Sand Canyon area. Unfortunately, it is rare to see horseback riding on the trails these days. However, we are expecting that horseback riding will be revitalized and tradition can be revived if we actively promote horseback riding to the resort guests. In fact, my daughter Elizabeth liked horseback riding when she was a child, so I used to take her to Burbank every weekend for horseback riding. This could be a tremendous opportunity for young children to have this experience while staying at the resort.

Eco-friendly resort

In the last few years, there have been extreme droughts in California, but unlike other regions, the SCV Water Division let residents know that the Santa Clarita area has well-equipped water reservoirs. This doesn't mean that we should not preserve water! We plan to filter the shower water used by guests and use it as irrigation water to water the plants. When it rains, we will collect, store and recycle the storm water and use it for the golf course irrigation.

By installing solar panels on the roofs of buildings and shades with solar panels on a portion of the parking lots, electrical energy used by the resort can be significantly reduced.

Along the way, I learned that most construction materials could be prefabricated outside the factory and assembled on the construction site. Cold formed steel for framing, bathroom, bars, doors, window and custom furniture could be ordered in advance and they could be brought in a timely manner and be installed on site expeditiously. Unlike ordinary construction, this is simpler and cleaner and it eliminates many uncertainties you might encounter during construction. More importantly, construction time can be significantly reduced.

Resorts for the community

I didn't even think about resort development when I first took over the golf course. Once I started, it was a new challenge for me and it made my heart beat with excitement and hope. It was a complex process as if we were painting on a white canvas and trying to create a timeless beautiful art piece. We hope the Sand Canyon Resort will become a recognized destination cherished for its natural setting, architecture and 5-star services.

Once the resort is built after a lot of effort and hard work, we hope that the local residents, LA county residents and even those from other states will enjoy the benefits of staying here: rejuvenate, spend time with family and friends, play golf, enjoy fine dining in the stress free natural setting in Sand Canyon.

In addition, a few hundred jobs will be created for local residents. I am convinced that many employees and their families could enjoy a stable life, which in turn will stimulate the local economy. Starting a new business is never easy. Nevertheless, creating a lot of jobs, especially in the community one cares for, is always very exciting and rewarding!

Every resort needs a lot of staff to work in various departments. The closest example, Ojai Valley Inn has about 700 employees. We plan to hire a few hundred employees including a staff of a few dozen chefs, which will be a great opportunity for those with culinary education from Canyon Country College.

In fact, there are many people who commute from Santa Clarita to Los Angeles, taking more than an hour and a half each way. If they could work at our resort, they would spend less time in traffic and hopefully could be much happier!

Currently, there aren't too many restaurants or other amenities for the Canyon Country residents. However, once the resort is opened, they could enjoy various kinds of fine dining, fitness, spa, sports and so on without having to go far.

We learned that the prices of houses in the Sand Canyon area are still relatively low compared to other places with similar sizes. I think this is because the Sand Canyon area is not well known to the people who live in Los Angeles. In fact, although Ojai is much more isolated, property prices are somewhat higher. I think this is because it has been discovered by Ojai Valley resort guests. When our resort becomes a local attraction, the price of real estate could certainly be appreciated.

Even When I lived in LA for many years and went to Mammoth or Yosemite, I just drove right by and didn't know such a beautiful place existed. It is a hidden jewel!

Design process

In February 2018, the Sand Canyon Resort & Spa development plan which took nine months of preparation was submitted to the City of Santa Clarita. While it was being reviewed by the City, we kept on working in detail with architects and making improvements.

At the start of the project, all designs were drawn in 2 dimensions (2D) by a software called AutoCAD. However, by looking at those drawings, I couldn't visualize how the resort would look. When I became frustrated with it, I found that there was a 3D architectural design tool called Revit.

The Revit could start the floor plan in 2D and build the elevations in 3D. Now I could visualize the actual buildings and rotate around to see from different angles. It could be transformed easily from the construction drawing, which could minimize errors during the construction phase.

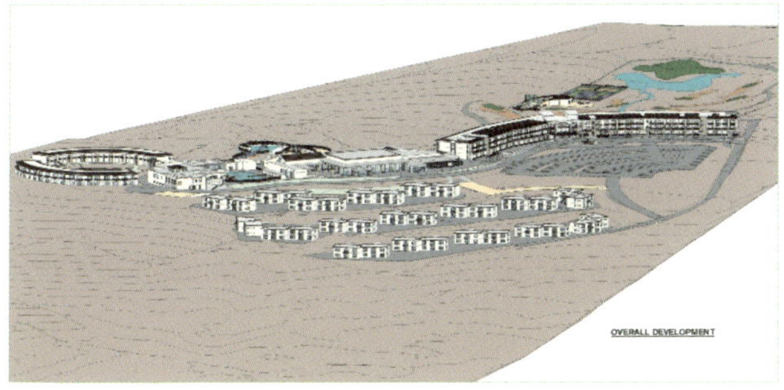

Actual 3D image

After many inquiries, I found an architectural company in San Diego who was using Revit. Being able to visualize the resort better, we had to make many changes to the previous design. My wife and I went down to San Diego every week so that architects could focus more on my project.

I learned from them about a new construction technology called Cold-Formed Steel (CFS) framing. Unlike the conventional construction method, the light gauge steel frame could be prefabricated at the factory according to the drawing and could be assembled on the construction site.

I was told that it could be built within 3 months. The construction could be much simpler and could save a few months of construction time. It could also minimize the construction noise time which could annoy the nearby residents. In addition, steel is free from fire hazard and is strong enough to withstand typhoons and earthquakes.

Two months after submitting the project plan to the City, I received feedback from the agencies involved. I learned that the grading requires bringing in more than 10,000 trucks of soil from outside. I found that it could cause a lot issues related to environmental impact. We revised the design so that we could balance the soil amount on site without bringing it in from outside. We also made changes to the site plan so we could save almost all oak trees.

In the course of the new design, we added a three-story spa garden inn next to the spa building. By doing that, we could increase the hotel rooms to 325 while decreasing the number of villas.

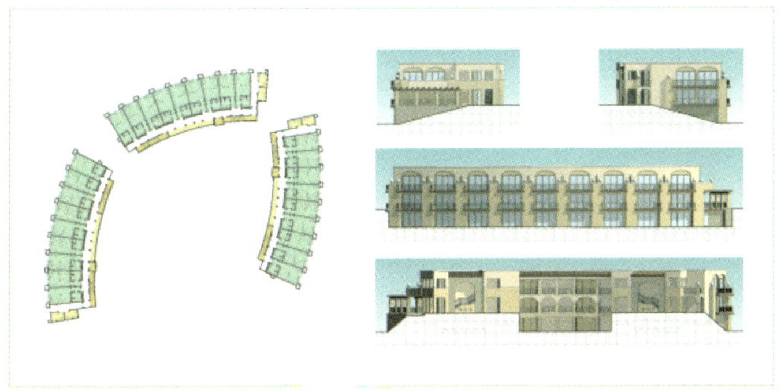

Spa Garden Inn - 81 junior suits

The city hired CBRE, a consulting company which specialized in conducting the business viability. They confirmed that the number of hotel rooms and the villa rooms are properly balanced. With all those changes made, we had to resubmit the overall plan again in October 2018.

Santa Clarita Cultural Center

On a casual occasion, I had dinner with Bill Miranda, one of the members of the Santa Clarita City Council.

"Bill, what is your new initiative after being reelected as a councilman?"

"Steve, I had a vision to build a Cultural Center for a while. I want to create a space that introduces not only our local traditions but also other cultures such as Native Americans, Central and South America."

"Is that right? Have you thought about where and how big?"

"I have not decided on a place yet, but I have a plan in mind and I have visited several cultural centers in different areas. I think the scale should be about 10,000 sf. and I'm looking for a suitable site near Newhall."

"If you set up a cultural center, you should have a lot of visitors. No matter how good a museum or exhibition hall is, there will be no meaning if there are only a few visitors."

"You are right."

"Bill, how many people will visit the cultural center if they are in downtown? We have about 30 acres of open space left over after the development, and I was wondering what the land could be used for."

"Steve, do you mean you're going to offer the site to the City?"

"It would be a wonderful place to build a cultural center surrounded by the botanical garden. It will become a monument for the City of Santa Clarita."

"Steve, what a great idea! I will drive the project right away."

The discussions I had with Bill were very meaningful to me. The resort, along with the cultural center, began to feel a sense of harmony and became another attraction. The number of people looking for a museum or exhibits are extremely limited, but it is much easier for the general public to access the museum by placing it in the resort.

We put our heads together and began to discuss how we should start building. I thought it could be a good idea to build a small outdoor stage in the original ecological park. With ideas for tourists, local communities and students in mind, ideas such as a main exhibition hall, A/V room, library, community room, and class room to learn culture and arts academy came about.

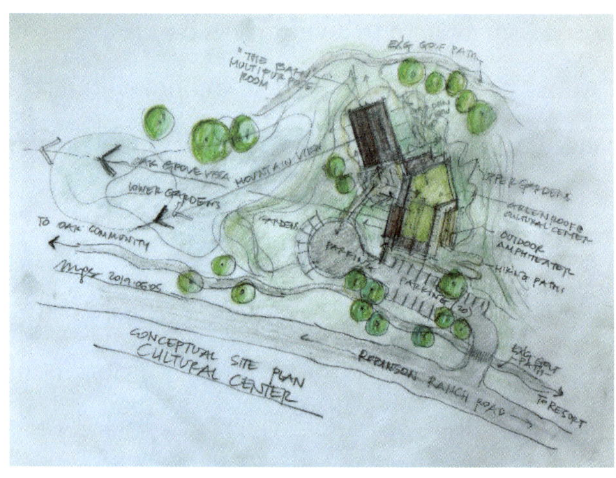

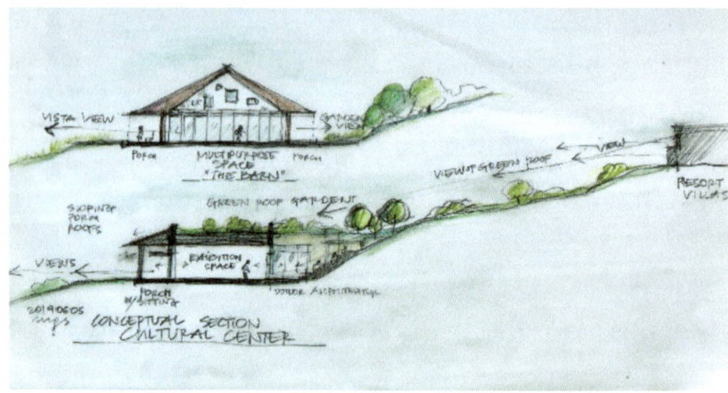

The providence of God

Looking back on my past life, it was a series of events that I didn't plan for myself and could not have accomplished without God's blessings. I was able to escape miraculously from unavoidable situations and critical moments.

There was my childhood when I was ashamed of being born into a poor house, but poverty and lacking things became the driving force for living fiercely.

I was able to go to America to pursue an American dream through my older sister who married an American. Moving from a large company to a small company where I was given an opportunity to start my own venture was not possible without God's intervention.

The difficulties that I experienced while running the two companies could never be overcome by my own strength.

Every time, there were miracle-like helping hands. I returned to Korea in 2007 after 30 years of American life because I was unhappy with money and success alone.

I published an autobiographical book by chance and started DHF leadership camp in 2009. However, when I was in trouble expanding the business, I met my current wife, Grace, and was able to grow it exponentially with her making it the most influential program in Korea.

Since the day Grace joined my team, she always exceeded my expectations no matter what type of work she did. With her experience teaching and a master's degree in industrial design, she helped me design the resort. She also helped with office and accounting work for the golf course. In particular, her devotion to the youth was a good fit for the work I was doing. I'm very grateful to my wife who still travels between U.S. and Korea to take care of our foundation and education business.

How lucky am I to be with someone who I can share and discuss my new ideas with! My wife is so gracious to always lend an open ear and advise me wisely. My encounter with my wife, who meets all my needs, is a precious gift in the providence of God.

Lucky double rainbow

Epilogue

In 2016, I happened to take over the golf course in Sand Canyon and moved back to the United States. After about two years of hard work, we restored the golf course and it is now stable enough for our employees to manage it on their own. I think it is no coincidence that I have found a new passion through the development of a resort. I believe that it was one of God's plans, as if each important opportunity was a piece of a puzzle.

Through the Sand Canyon Country Club, I became familiar with the locals and now it is like second home where I plan to spend the rest of my life. Two years ago, Bob Kellar, who served as a member of the Santa Clarita City Council for more than 20 years, came to our golf course. During my conversation with him, I learned that he was very involved with local veterans and many non-profit organizations. Later, I went to the 'Triumph Foundation Annual Fundraising Event' with him.

Since then, I've been involved in a number of other non-profit organizations that need financial support such as the Senior Center, Henry Mayo Hospital, College of Canyons Foundation, Michael Hoefflin Foundation, Boys & Girls Club, Salvation Army, YMCA, Bridge to the home, Soroptimist International, Domestic Violence Center of SCV. I was able to provide financial support to these groups and through this participation, I had the opportunity to interact with many people.

The Sand Canyon Resort may be my last venture. I'm investing all my passion into it, such that all our guests are able to make happy memories and the residents can be proud of this new landmark in Santa Clarita. However, this is not something I can do alone. It is only possible when the neighbors and people involved in this project understand my pure intentions and become partners.

In retrospect, it is a miracle that a young man from a poor country has achieved such success with his bare hands in foreign lands. It was only possible because the United States gave a fair opportunity to all the immigrants. I want to use the rest of my life to use the blessings I have received.

Many immigrants are still dreaming of various American dreams. As one of the citizens of the United States, I applaud and will support their challenges.

Finally, I want to thank my niece, Diane, who was willing to translate for me while she was busy raising her two children and taking care of her husband.